STUDENT'S BOOK

English 2 Explorer

Helen Stephenson

NATIONAL GEOGRAPHIC LEARNING | CENGAGE Learning·

Australia • Brazil • Japan • Korea • Mexico • Singapore • Spain • United Kingdom • United States

Contents

Skills: Listening & Speaking	Working with words / Study Skills / Pronunciation		Culture & CLIL
Listening: Classroom language Speaking: Giving personal information	Working with words:	nouns and verbs	
Listening: An interview Speaking: Making suggestions Talking about likes and dislikes	Working with words: Study skills: Pronunciation:	verb + -ing using a dictionary (1) syllables	The Notting Hill Carnival CLIL: Music and English Musical instruments
Listening: A Mongolian teenager Speaking: Making phone calls Leaving phone messages	Working with words: Study skills: Pronunciation:	verb + on/off -er nouns from verbs using a dictionary (2) -ed endings	Wild Canada CLIL: Chemistry and English Crystals
Listening: An interview Speaking: Expressing and asking for opinions Agreeing and disagreeing	Working with words: Study skills: Pronunciation:	time expressions -ing/-ed adjectives predicting -ed endings	American icons CLIL: History and English The New World
Listening: A story Speaking: Making and accepting apologies	Working with words: Study skills: Pronunciation:	time expressions reading - new words /ae/, /e/ and /ɜː/	Australian stories CLIL: Maths and English Interpreting diagrams
Listening: An interview Speaking: Buying things in shops	Working with words: Study skills: Pronunciation:	adjectives + too/ enough learning new words intonation in questions with question words	Southern Africa: desert and delta CLIL: Geography and English The continents
Listening: A food expert Speaking: Asking for and giving permission	Working with words: Study skills: Pronunciation:	-tion nouns from verbs learning new grammatical forms final /s/ and /z/ sounds	Extreme New Zealand CLIL: Biology and English Oxygen and exercise
Listening: Experiences Speaking: Asking for and giving advice	Working with words: Study skills: Pronunciation:	compound nouns independent learning (1) silent letters	The bog bodies of Ireland CLIL: Social science and English The European Union
Listening: Holiday arrangements Speaking: Asking for and giving directions	Working with words: Study skills: Pronunciation:	prepositions of location independent learning (2) three-syllable words	School holidays in the UK CLIL: Geography and English Maps

Kate

Judy

1 Look at the photo of Kate and Judy at school. Which of these things can you see? Compare with your partner.

> a bag   a board   a CD player   a chair
> a clock   a corrector pen   a desk   a dictionary
> a DVD   a highlighter   a notebook   a pen
> a pencil   a rubber   a ruler   a sheet of paper
> a timetable   a wall   a window   a workbook

2 Which things in Exercise 1 can you see in your classroom? Take turns to say a word and point to the thing.

3 Work in pairs. Which of the things in Exercise 1 are classroom objects? Which are your personal items? Write the words in two groups.

Classroom objects	Personal items
a board	a bag

4 (•S1 Listen and check your answers to Exercise 3. Repeat.

5 Work in pairs. Ask and answer questions about the personal things in Exercise 3.

> e.g. A: *Have you got a red bag*
>   B: *Yes, I have. / No, I haven't.*

6 Complete the sentences with *in* or *on*.

1 The book is .... the desk.
2 Our bags are .... the floor.
3 I've got a pen .... my pocket.
4 The exercises are .... the board.
5 Have you got a ruler .... your bag?

7 Write true sentences with the affirmative or negative form of *be* or *have got*.

1 Our classroom .... room 6.
2 I .... fourteen years old.
3 I .... a notebook in my bag.
4 My bag .... black and grey.
5 We .... a new timetable.

See Grammar Explorer: Page 122

Lewis

Adam

8 S2 **Listen to Lewis and Adam talking about their timetable. Complete the timetable with words from the box.**

art   biology   chemistry   English
French   geography   history   IT
maths   music   PE   physics

	Mon	Tues
9.00	English	history
9.50		(3) ....
10.40	break	
11.00	(1)	PE
11.50	maths	maths
12.40	lunch	
1.55	(2)	(4) ....
14.45	art	

9 **Work in pairs. Draw your school timetable. Write the days, times and subjects in English. Use your dictionary if necessary.**

Monday   Tuesday   Wednesday
Thursday   Friday

10 **Test your partner. Take turns.**

e.g. **A:** *What's on Tuesday at ten to twelve?*
  B: *English?*
  A: *No!*

Project

Work in pairs. Find out about your school. How many classrooms / students / teachers has it got? Has it got a library / a playground / a sports field / a science laboratory / a dining room / a hall? Write at least six sentences about your school.

1 Work in pairs. Can you translate these useful classroom expressions into your language?

USEFUL EXPRESSIONS

Can I borrow a pencil?
Can you help me?
What does … mean?
How do you spell … ?
Can I go to the toilet, please?

2 Work in pairs. Write responses for the expressions in Exercise 1. Then practise with your partner.

e.g. **A:** *Can I borrow a pencil?*
 B: *Yes, of course.*

3 Work in pairs. Do the English Explorer 2 quiz. Compare your answers with a new partner.

English Explorer 2 Quiz

True or false?

1 There are eight units in *English Explorer 2*.
2 There's a story about a boy and a lion on page 44.
3 There isn't a Video worksheet after Unit 1.
4 There's a Vocabulary section after Unit 8.
5 There's a Grammar section in this book.
6 There aren't any photos of Lewis and Adam in Unit 6.
7 There are four True Story pages in this book.
8 There are two Review sections in this book.

4 Write true sentences about your class. Use the affirmative or negative form of *There is / There are*.

1 .... thirty students in our class.
2 .... a board on the wall.
3 .... a computer in our classroom.
4 .... pictures on the walls.
5 .... one door in this classroom.

See Grammar Explorer: Page 122

5 🔊 S3 **Listen to Adam and Lewis, and look at the questionnaire. Circle the number of the questions Adam asks. What are Lewis's responses (✓ or ✗)?**

Can you … ?	Lewis	Your partner
1 count to 100 in English		
2 cook a meal		
3 copy information to a CD		
4 name three school subjects in English		
5 drive a car		
6 sing a song in English		
7 ride a bike		
8 tell the time in English		

6 Look at your answers for Exercise 5. Are the sentences true or false?

1 Lewis can't cook a meal.
2 Lewis can copy information to a CD.
3 Lewis can drive a car.
4 Lewis can ride a bike.

See Grammar Explorer: Page 122

7 Work in pairs. Use the questionnaire in Exercise 5. Find out about your partner.

e.g. **A:** *Can you count to 100 in English?*
 B: *Yes, I can.*

8 Write six sentences with the results of your survey.

e.g. *Maria can count to 100 in English.*

Working with words

9 Look through two units of *English Explorer 2*. Where are the *Working with words* exercises?

10 Do this *Working with words* exercise. Find the missing words on pages 6–7 and complete the table.

Noun	
	express
help	
meaning	
	inform
	list
	respond
spelling	
translation	

Fast finishers

Look through *English Explorer 2*. Where are the Fast finishers activities?

Do this one now: Close your book. Write a list of classroom objects in English. How many can you name? Then open your book at page 4 and check your list.

Here is another activity: Put the words in the box into four groups. How many other words can you add to the group?

art	black	eight	English	Friday
grey	music	nine	red	Saturday
ten	Wednesday			

1 Read about the four friends. Find two mistakes in each description. Then write the correct sentences.

1 Kate and her friends are in Kate's house. Kate's wearing a red T-shirt and a shirt. She's got an apple in her hand. Judy's wearing a white shirt. She's got a bottle of water in her hand. Kate and Judy have got dark hair. Kate and Judy are happy.

2 Adam's got short hair. He's wearing grey trousers and white trainers. His bag is on the floor. It's black. Adam's got some crisps.

3 Lewis is slim and he's got fair hair. He's wearing jeans and a shirt. His shirt is white. He hasn't got a drink.

Remember that the apostrophe 's can mean is (*Adam's tall*), has (*Adam's got a drink*) or it can be the possessive form (*Adam's bag is black*).

2 Write *is*, *has* or *possessive* for each sentence.

1 Kate's got an apple.
2 Judy's shirt is white.
3 Kate's happy.
4 Lewis's hair is long.
5 Adam's wearing grey trousers.

See Grammar Explorer: Page 122

3 Complete the sentences with the correct possessive adjective.

1 This is my friend. .... name's Frieda.
2 Frieda and I are in the same class and .... houses are in the same street.
3 That's the maths teacher. .... name's Mr Brown.
4 Kate and Judy are with .... friends.
5 Can I borrow .... book, please?

See Grammar Explorer: Page 122

Study skills

Using a vocabulary notebook

The **Study skills** exercises in *English Explorer 2* help you organise your learning. For example, look again at Exercise 3 on page 4. Writing words in groups is a good idea for your vocabulary notebook. Now write the clothes from Exercise 1 on the opposite page in these groups.

Formal   Informal
shirt   T-shirt

4 **Write about somebody in your class. Don't write the person's name. Read your partner's paragraph. Can you identify the person?**

   e.g. This person is ....

5 S4 **Listen to the conversation and tick (✓) the words you hear.**

   aunt   brother   cousin   dad
   grandfather   grandmother   grandparents
   mum   parents   sister   uncle

6 S4 **Listen again and write the countries you hear. Who is from each country? Compare with your partner.**

7 **Write five sentences about people in your family. Write their names, where they are from, and where they live now. Have you got any family in an English-speaking country?**

8 S5 **Kate goes to join Adam's sports club. Listen to the conversation and complete the form.**

Birchwood Sports Association

1 Name   Kate

2 Surname   ....

3 Address   ....

4 Post code   ....

5 Telephone number   247685

6 Age   fourteen

9 S5 **Work in pairs. Look at the form again and write the receptionist's questions. Then listen again and check.**

   e.g. What's your name?

10 **Work in pairs. Ask and answer the questions from Exercise 9.**

   e.g. A: *What's your name?*
        B: *My name's ...*

11 **Look at the questionnaire and write sentences.**

What's your favourite … ?	
food	My favourite food is ...
sport	
film	
band	
school subject	
book	

12 **Work with other people in the class. Find someone who has got the same favourite things as you. Tell the class.**

   e.g. *My favourite food is pasta and it's John's favourite food too.*

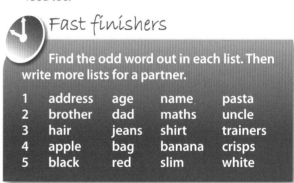

Fast finishers

Find the odd word out in each list. Then write more lists for a partner.

1	address	age	name	pasta
2	brother	dad	maths	uncle
3	hair	jeans	shirt	trainers
4	apple	bag	banana	crisps
5	black	red	slim	white

I can...

I can talk about people and clothes.
I can talk about my family.
I can give personal information.
I can talk about my favourite things.
I can use possessive forms.

Classroom language: teacher

- Copy these words in your notebook.
- Do you understand?
- Read Exercise 4 silently.
- Listen to me.
- Don't talk, please.
- Do Exercise 5 for homework.
- Look at the board.
- Open your notebooks / your books at page 11.
- Write in your notebooks.

Classroom language: student

- Can I borrow a pen / rubber / pencil?
- Can you help me?
- Finished.
- Can I go to the toilet, please?
- Excuse me. I don't understand.
- What does ... mean, please?

Exercise instructions

1 Are the sentences true or false?
2 Ask and answer questions.
3 Choose the correct words.
4 Compare with your partner.
5 Complete the sentences.
6 Find the people in the photo.
7 Listen and check.
8 Listen and repeat.
9 Listen. Write the words you hear.
10 Look at the pictures.
11 Match the questions with the answers.
12 Put the words in order to make questions.
13 Read and listen to the dialogue.
14 Read the dialogue again. Complete the table.
15 Read the text.
16 Study the table.
17 Take turns.
18 Use your dictionary.
19 Work in pairs.
20 Write sentences with these words.

Free time

> Grammar

Learn about the present simple, and adverbs of frequency.

> Vocabulary

Learn words for interests and activities, and performing.

> Skills

Read about student profiles, a festival in Papua New Guinea, and the Notting Hill Carnival.

Listen to an interview with a performer on a TV programme.

Write a personal profile.

> Communicate

Make suggestions, and talk about likes and dislikes.

1 Work in pairs. What can you see in the photo?

2 1.1 Listen. What does the girl like doing?

  a drawing

  b playing the piano

  c meeting friends

3 Write three things you like doing in your free time.

See Vocabulary Explorer: Page 98

4 Work in pairs and compare your lists. What have you got in common?

Student profiles

Reading and listening

1 1.2 **Read and listen to the information about two students – Fekria and Jamie. Complete the sentences with the correct names.**

e.g. *Fekria's* favourite subjects are reading and sports.

1 There are 600 students at …………'s school.

2 After school, ………… helps at home.

3 ………… is the first student in her family.

4 ………… likes skateboarding.

5 …………'s ambition is to be a doctor.

2 **Read about another student. Complete the notes about Will.**

Will is 14. He goes to Broadfield Junior High School in London. Will likes English and music. He plays the drums in the school orchestra. There are about 1,500 students in Will's school. They are all 11–18 years old. The boys and the girls study the same subjects. They don't have different classes. Broadfield Junior High School is an old school – it's 100 years old this year. Will's parents and grandparents are ex-students. In the evening, Will doesn't think about school and homework. He meets his friends or practises the drums. He loves playing drums in the orchestra. His ambition is to be a professional musician.

Age: 14
Favourite subjects: …………
Number of students at school: …………
Year of school construction: …………
Generations of family as students: *three*
After-school activities: …………
Ambition: …………

Age
13 / 13

Favourite subjects
Reading and sports / Maths and art

Number of students at school
218 (all girls) / 600 (boys and girls)

Year of school construction
2002 / 1875

Generations of family as students
She's the first / Four

After-school activities
Helps her mother with housework /
Skateboarding, homework, TV

Ambition
To be a doctor / To be an athlete
and to represent Australia in the Olympics

Fekria Abdul Saboor from
Kabul, Afghanistan

Jamie Turner from
Brisbane, Australia

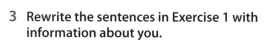

3 **Rewrite the sentences in Exercise 1 with information about you.**

e.g. *My favourite subjects are* ……

4 **Work in pairs and compare your sentences. What have you got in common?**

Grammar: present simple

5 **Complete the tables with the words in the box.**

| do | does | doesn't | don't | goes | study |

Affirmative	
I/You/We/They	(**1**) ………… the same subjects.
He/She/It	(**2**) ………… to school.
Negative	
I/You/We/They	(**3**) ………… have different classes.
He/She/It	(**4**) ………… think about school.

Remember the spelling changes: *go – goes, study – studies, watch – watches.*

Questions		
(5) .... Does	I/you/we/they he/she/it	live in London?
Short answers		
Yes,	I/you/we/they he/she/it	do. (6) ....
No,	I/you/we/they he/she/it	don't. doesn't.

See Grammar Explorer: Page 123

6 Complete the sentences with the present simple form of the verbs.

e.g. Fekria *helps* her mother at home. (**help**)

1 My brother .... to university. (**go**)

2 I .... maths. (**not like**)

3 My friends .... after school. (**meet**)

4 Jamie .... TV after school. (**watch**)

5 Will .... his homework every night. (**not do**)

7 Write questions with the words. Then work in pairs. Ask and answer the questions. Take turns.

e.g. Fekria / like sports? *Does Fekria like sports?*

1 Jamie / live in London?

2 boys / study at Fekria's school?

3 Will / play the drums?

4 you / like school?

5 you / help your parents?

8 Work in pairs. Ask and answer questions about the pictures.

e.g. A: *Does she play the guitar?*

B: *No, she doesn't.*

1 she / play the guitar?   2 he / like football?

3 they / live in London?   4 they / go to school?

5 she / study music?   6 he / wear school uniform?

Working with words

9 Look at the examples. Then make words for activities from the verbs.

e.g. cycle: Her favourite activity is cycling.
play: He likes playing the drums.

> cycle   play   dance   draw
> meet (friends)   paint   sing
> skateboard   study   swim
> watch (TV)

> Remember the spelling changes: *cycle – cycling, swim – swimming.*

Vocabulary

10 Complete the sentence with *-ing* words.

1 I like .... English. It's one of my favourite subjects.

2 We've got four bikes in my family. We love ....

3 My parents hate .... TV.

4 I don't like .... very much. The water gets in my eyes.

5 My best friend loves .... She goes to ballet classes after school.

6 I can't play an instrument, but I love .... songs.

11 Write true sentences about yourself with interest or activity words.

I like …

I love …

I don't like …

I hate …

See Vocabulary Explorer: Page 98

12 Work in pairs. Ask and answer questions. Use *like / love / hate.*

e.g. A: *Do you like music?*

B: *Yes, I do. I love Eminem and …*

Fast finishers

How many free-time activities and interests can you name? Write a list. Then work in pairs and compare your lists. Who has got more words?

The Sing-Sing festival in Papua New Guinea

Reading and listening

1 **Work in pairs. Look at the photos and discuss the questions. What do you think?**

1 Does the boy paint his face every morning?

2 Do the people wear these costumes every day?

2 🔊 **1.3 Read and listen to the text. Check your answers to Exercise 1.**

3 **Read the text again. Are the sentences true or false?**

1 A Sing-Sing is a cultural festival.

2 People in Papua New Guinea meet every weekend.

3 Men usually hunt and cook.

4 Boys often spend long periods in the forest.

August is a special month in the capital of Papua New Guinea, Mount Hagen. The Sing-Sing is in August. It's a weekend of spectacular dancing, singing and telling stories.

The people of Papua New Guinea live in about 1,000 tribal groups all over the country. They don't often meet, but the Sing-Sing is a special occasion. Hundreds of people take part in the festival. Different groups wear different costumes. They paint their bodies with patterns in beautiful colours. The groups have competitions. They dance, they play the drums, and they act dramatic stories. The judges decide the winners.

Day-to-day life is very different – men usually hunt animals or work on the land. Women cook and look after their children. Families don't meet every day because they never live together in the same house. Boys live with their mothers until they are about ten years old. Then they go to their father's house. They often spend long periods of time in the forest. Girls and young children always help their mothers.

At the Sing-Sing, people always make new friends. It's always a fantastic weekend for the performers and for the audience.

Grammar: adverbs of frequency

4 Complete the table with adverbs of frequency from the text on the opposite page.

100% ....

↑ usually

....

sometimes

0% ....

See Grammar Explorer: Page 123

> Adverbs of frequency go before main verbs in affirmative and negative sentences, but after *be*:
> *Girls always help their mothers.*
> *It's always a fantastic weekend.*

5 Write true sentences about yourself with adverbs of frequency. Use these ideas.

e.g. *I often meet my friends at weekends.*

- meet / friends / weekends
- have / pizza / dinner
- go / cinema / family
- walk / school
- play / computer games / evening
- help / housework
- have / birthday party / restaurant
- tidy / bedroom / weekends

6 Work in pairs. How well do you know your partner? How often does he/she do the things in exercise 5?

e.g. A: *You never meet your friends at weekends.*
B: *False. I often meet my friends at weekends.*
A: *You often have pizza for dinner.*
B: *True.*

Listening

7 ◉ 1.4 **Listen to an interview with Ellie, a performer on the TV show *The X Factor*. Write the days Ellie does these things.**

e.g. *singing lessons Mondays and ....*

acting classes

dance group

concerts

music festivals

8 ◉ 1.4 **Listen to the interview again. What does Ellie want to do?**

> act in a film
> act in a play
> dance in a show
> do magic
> perform in a circus
> play an instrument
> sing in a concert
> take part in a festival

See Vocabulary Explorer: Page 99

9 Answer the questions for yourself. Then work in pairs and ask your partner. Take turns.

> often   sometimes   never

How often do you … ?

go to a concert

play an instrument

sing

wear make up

dance

wear a costume

act in a play

perform in public

Study skills

Using a dictionary (1)

1 Write these words in alphabetical order.

> young   housework   athlete   swim
> homework   acting   yellow
> skateboarding   school   students

2 Find the words above in your dictionary. Work in pairs and race your partner.

Making suggestions

Reading and listening

1 🔘 1.5 **Read and listen to the dialogue. Which club does Kate decide to join?**

1	the chess club	
2	the choir	
3	the magic circle club	
4	the photography club	
5	the school orchestra	
6	the theatre group	

2 **Find these ways of making suggestions in the dialogue.**

Why don't you + verb?
Let's + verb.
How about + noun?
How about + verb+'ing'?

Adam: Hey, Judy!

Judy: Hello, Adam. Hi, Lewis. This is my friend Kate.

Adam: Hi, Kate. We're in the theatre group – do you like acting?

Kate: Yes, I do. I love acting!

Adam: Well, why don't you join our club? We meet every Wednesday at four o'clock.

Kate: OK, great idea!

Judy: Where do you meet?

Lewis: In room seven. See you on Wednesday!

Kate: OK. Let's find a club for you, Judy.

Lewis: What do you like doing? How about photography?

Judy: Are you crazy? My photos are terrible!

Adam: Well, how about joining the school orchestra?

Judy: But I can't play an instrument!

Kate: That's true.

Judy: Hey, look! The magic circle club – I love magic!

Kate: Oh, yes!

Judy: Let's go to their table. Come on.

3 🔊 1.6 **Listen to three suggestions. Choose the correct response.**

1 a But I don't like acting.
   b Yes, I do.
   c Sorry, I can't play the drums.

2 a Great! I'm really hungry!
   b Good idea! I love taking photos.
   c No, it's not my camera.

3 a Sorry, but I don't like chess.
   b Yes, I love it.
   c Great idea!

4 🔊 1.7 **Listen and repeat the *Useful expressions*. Focus on your intonation.**

USEFUL EXPRESSIONS

Why don't you join our club?
Let's go to their table.
How about photography?
How about joining the school orchestra?
OK, great idea!
You're joking!
But I can't play the piano.

Speaking

5 **Work in pairs. You've got free time on Tuesday afternoons. Suggest some activities. Use the ideas in Exercise 1 and the *Useful expressions*. Take turns.**

e.g. A: *Do you like singing?*
        B: *Yes, I do.*
        A: *Well, why don't you …*

Pronunciation: syllables

6 🔊 1.8 **Say each word. How many syllables has it got? Then listen, check and repeat.**

> ambition   festival   friend   homework
> subject   weekend

Writing: a personal profile

1 **Read Adam's profile on an international student website. Find out these things about him.**

1 age
2 school
3 favourite subjects
4 free-time interests
5 ambition
6 weak points
7 good points

2 **Look at the profile again. Rewrite the pairs of sentences (1–3) as one sentence.**

e.g. I like playing football. + I like taking photos.
        = I like playing football and taking photos.

1 Click on my photo. Write to me.
2 I love magic. I love photography.
3 I love singing. I'm in the choir.

3 **Make notes about yourself. Use the categories in Exercise 1. Then write your profile. Refer to Adam's profile and Exercise 2 for help.**

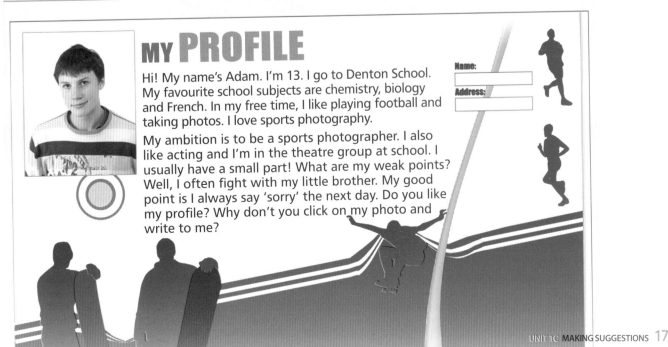

E-mail

MY PROFILE

Hi! My name's Adam. I'm 13. I go to Denton School. My favourite school subjects are chemistry, biology and French. In my free time, I like playing football and taking photos. I love sports photography.

My ambition is to be a sports photographer. I also like acting and I'm in the theatre group at school. I usually have a small part! What are my weak points? Well, I often fight with my little brother. My good point is I always say 'sorry' the next day. Do you like my profile? Why don't you click on my photo and write to me?

Name:

Address:

Reading

1 Work in pairs. What do you know about carnivals? Tell your partner.

2 🔊 1.9 **Read the text and answer the questions about the Notting Hill Carnival.**

1 Where is Notting Hill?
2 When is the carnival?
3 Who takes part in the carnival?

3 **Read the text again and find four adjectives which describe the carnival.**

4 **Read the text again and find seven things that people do before and at the carnival.**

Culture

UK

Trinidad

My family lives in Notting Hill in London. My dad's family is from Trinidad in the Caribbean. There are a lot of people here in the UK with connections to Trinidad. We've got friends and family in both places. Every year, at the end of August, people organise a big carnival – the Notting Hill Carnival. It's like the carnivals in Trinidad. Different groups spend months in preparation. They make spectacular costumes, and practise dances and music. The music is special. It's steel band and calypso music, and it's originally from Trinidad. The carnival parades through the streets of London and everyone joins in. Families, friends and even the police enjoy the music and the dancing. It's great!

Listening

5 ● 1.10 **Listen to a student from London talking about playing in a steel band. Choose the correct answers.**

1 The instruments are
   a wooden drums.
   b metal drums.
   c paper drums.

2 The band practises
   a every day.
   b on Saturday and Sunday.
   c in summer.

3 The band gives concerts
   a all year.
   b in winter.
   c in summer.

4 People in the audience often
   a sing.
   b dance.
   c clap.

5 The band .... plays at the Notting Hill Carnival.
   a always
   b usually
   c sometimes

Project

Choose a festival that you know about. Find or draw pictures and make a poster for the festival.

When is the festival?

Where is the festival?

Who takes part in the festival?

What happens at the festival?

Music and English
Musical instruments

1 Do you know the names of these instruments in English? Read about different groups of instruments. Match the words in red with the pictures.

There are different groups of musical instruments. They include string, wind, percussion and keyboard instruments.

String instruments
String instruments include the violin, the harp and the guitar. The violin and the harp are often part of an orchestra. Violins have four strings. There are different sizes of harp – some have 46 strings!

Wind instruments
This group includes woodwind and brass instruments such as the flute, the saxophone and the trumpet. These are classical music instruments, but cultures all around the world also have different types of wind instruments. To play these instruments, you blow them.

Percussion instruments
It's easy to make a percussion instrument. You can hit a metal drum with a stick to make music – that's a percussion instrument. The xylophone and all the different types of drums are percussion instruments.

Electronic instruments
You can often hear electronic keyboards and synthesisers in modern and pop music.

2 ● 1.11 **Listen to the instruments and write the numbers.**

   e.g. _saxophone 1_

violin	guitar	saxophone	xylophone
harp	flute	trumpet	drums

4Real

4REAL

http://www.4real.com/

REAL People. REAL Places. REAL Stories. REAL Change.

Home | 4REAL TV Series | Community | Action | Marketplace | Search

Email | Password | Save | login | join

AS TEENAGERS

Sol Guy and Josh Thome go to school together at Grand Forks, Canada. They are good friends, but their interests are quite different. Sol is into music, especially hip hop. He also likes studying business and economics. Josh is into the environment. He starts an Environmental Club at school.

AFTER SCHOOL

Sol works in the record industry. He continues his interest in hip hop music. He is the manager of big recording artists and a successful record industry executive. Josh works with youth movements. He focuses on both social and environmental change. His youth organisations develop internationally.

IN THEIR TWENTIES

They decide to work together. Their ambition is to use music and the Internet to help young people change their society and environment.

IN 2004

They create 4REAL. It's an online community and a TV programme. 4REAL takes celebrity artists like Joaquin Phoenix and Cameron Diaz to meet the leaders of community youth movements around the world. It helps people like MV Bill, a hip hop artist in Brazil. MV Bill also creates community centres for poor kids. 4REAL helps young people to learn from each other and helps young people finance their own projects.

You can read about 4REAL on the website and see it on National Geographic TV channels.

http://www.4real.com/
http://www.ngc.pl/

1 **Work in pairs and compare your answers to these questions.**

1 What kinds of music do young people like?

2 What kinds of problems do young people have?

3 How do young people communicate with each other?

2 **Read the text about National Geographic Emerging Explorers Sol Guy and Josh Thome, and answer the questions.**

1 Where are they from?

2 What are their interests?

3 What is their ambition?

3 **Read the text again and find information about 4REAL. What is it? Where can you see it?**

4 **Do young people help their communities in your town/country? What do they do? What do you do? Tell your class.**

Jobs and work

2

> Grammar

Learn about the present simple and the present continuous.

> Vocabulary

Learn words for describing weather, and for jobs.

> Skills

Read about a hurricane hunter, a Mongolian farmer's son, and Canada.

Listen to the story of farmers in Mongolia, and to answerphone messages.

Write a description of a person in a photo.

> Communicate

Make phone calls, and leave phone messages.

1   Work in pairs. Look at the photo. What do you think is happening?

2   2.1 Listen. Who is speaking?

   a   a doctor

   b   a fire fighter

   c   a police officer

See Vocabulary Explorer: Page 101

3   What is your ambition? What job do you want to do – or *not* want to do? Why? / Why not?

4   Tell your partner about your ambitions. Give your reasons.

Reading and listening

1 **Look at the photo. What do you think it shows? Choose one of the options.**

a   tsunamis
b   hurricanes
c   snowstorms

2 **2.2 Read and listen to the text. Are the sentences true or false?**

1   Rebecca is flying into a hurricane.
2   She is measuring the speed of the wind.
3   It's raining in the city.
4   People are leaving the city.

Reporter: It's Sunday morning here in New Orleans and Rebecca King is at work. She's a scientist – she studies the weather. Her job is sometimes dangerous. Rebecca is a 'hurricane hunter'. This morning, she's in a small plane over the sea. She and the pilot are flying over the Gulf of Mexico. She's studying Hurricane Katrina. Rebecca, what's the weather like at the moment?

Rebecca: Well, it's very scary! It's raining hard and it's really windy. The plane is bouncing up and down! I'm looking out of the window, to the east. They sky over the sea is very dark.

Reporter: Are you flying into the hurricane? What are you doing?

Rebecca: Well, yes we are! We're trying to find out the direction of the hurricane. We're measuring the speed and the direction of the wind. The wind is about 250 kilometres per hour right now. This is an enormous hurricane. It's coming to the coast. Is it raining in the city at the moment?

Reporter: No, it isn't. But it's very cloudy and windy. We're all preparing for the hurricane. People aren't staying in the city. They're leaving their homes and they're driving to safe areas. Some people are getting on buses and planes. Hurricane Katrina is coming!

Vocabulary

3 Read the dialogue again and find three expressions for the weather.

4 Match the words in the box with the pictures.

| cloudy | cold | foggy | hot | raining |
| snowing | sunny | windy | | |

See Vocabulary Explorer: Page 100

Grammar: present continuous

5 Look at the example. Read the dialogue again. Underline twelve more affirmative present continuous verbs.

e.g. Hurricane Katrina is coming.

6 Complete the tables with *is*, *isn't*, *are* and *aren't*.

Affirmative		
I	'm	looking out of the window.
He/She/It	(**1**)	coming to the coast.
We/You/They	(**2**)	leaving their homes.

Negative		
I	'm not	staying.
He/She/It	(**3**)	flying.
We/You/They	(**4**)	waiting.

Questions		
(**5**)	it	raining?
Is	he/she	staying?
(**6**)	we/you/they	flying?

Short answers		
Yes,	I	am.
	we/you/they	are.
	he/she/it	is.
No,	I	'm not.
	we/you/they	aren't.
	he/she/it	(**7**) ....

See Grammar Explorer: Page 123

7 Write a sentence for each picture. Use the present continuous form of the verbs.

e.g. They're putting up their umbrellas.

1 put up / umbrellas

2 put on / sun cream

3 turn on / car lights

4 take off / jumper

5 put on / gloves

6 hold on / to hats

8 Work in pairs. Ask and answer questions about the pictures in Exercise 7. Use the weather expressions in Exercise 4.

e.g. A: *Why are they putting up their umbrellas?*
B: *Because it's raining.*

9 Choose a location from the box and write four sentences. Then work in groups. Read your sentences to the group. Guess the location. Take turns.

e.g. A: *I'm sitting down. I'm listening to music. My dad is sitting next to me. I'm eating a sandwich.*
B: *Are you in a car?*
A: *Yes, I am. / No, I'm not.*

| on a bus | in a car | on a plane | at school |
| at home | in the garden | in Siberia | |

Working with words

10 Complete the verbs with *off* or *on*.

e.g. Get *on* the bus and sit down.

1 Take .... your shoes at the door.
2 It's dark! Turn .... the light.
3 Put your hat ....
4 It's an exam. Turn .... your mobile.
5 Let's put .... some music.
6 Get .... the bus at the next stop.

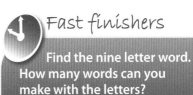

Fast finishers

Find the nine letter word. How many words can you make with the letters?

C	U	R
I	H	N
R	A	E

Listening

1 You are going to hear about a group of Mongolian farmers. They go on a difficult trip every autumn. Find these places on the map before you listen.

Darhad Valley	Lake Hovsgol

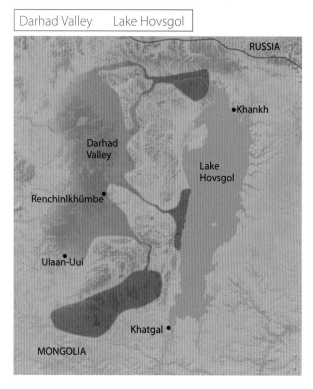

2 🔘 2.3 Listen and follow the direction of the trip on the map.

3 🔘 2.3 Listen again and answer the questions.

1 How many farmers go on the trip?
   a 1,000   **b** 2,000   **c** 10,000

2 How many animals go on the trip?
   a 6,000   **b** 16,000   **c** 60,000

3 How many kilometres do they travel?
   a 8   **b** 80   **c** 800

Reading and listening

4 🔘 2.4 Read and listen to the text about one of the Mongolian farming families. Match the correct heading (a-e) with each paragraph (1–4). There is one extra heading.

   a Uncle and his family
   b Morning activities
   c Bogii at school
   d A new camp
   e *Bogii and his family - 1*

5 Read and listen again. Who are the people in the photos?

1 Bogii lives in the Darhad Valley, in Mongolia. His family are farmers. They keep animals. Bogii is 13 years old. In October, he usually goes to school in the city. But this year is different – Bogii is helping his family with the autumn trip to Lake Hovsgol. It's a difficult trip and it takes many days. Bogii tells us about the trip.

2 'That's me. I'm wearing a hat and gloves because it's snowing. We're at a new camp. I'm putting up our 'tent'. It's called a ger. Every evening, I build the ger. My grandfather usually helps me, but he's ill at the moment. He isn't travelling with us. He's riding in a truck to Lake Hovsgol. '

3 'In this photo, I'm putting blankets onto the ox. Every morning, I pack our things. On the trip, I ride a horse and watch the animals with my dad. That's my dad behind me. He's wearing a yellow belt. My mum is in the ger. She's making a meal.'

4 'These are my cousins. They're travelling on an ox. They usually live in the city with my uncle. My uncle drives a truck for a tourism company. Right now, he's driving my grandfather to Lake Hovsgol.'

Grammar: present simple and present continuous

6 Read the sentences about Bogii and his family. Write *now* or *usually* for each one.

e.g. Bogii goes to school in the city. usually

1 Bogii is helping his family.
2 His mother is making a meal.
3 His grandfather helps Bogii.
4 His grandfather is riding in the truck.
5 His cousins live in the city.

See Grammar Explorer: Page 123

7 Choose the correct form of the verb.

e.g. 'Is your dad a doctor?'
'Yes, he **works** / is working at the hospital now.'

1 'Is Josh at work today?'
'Yes, he always **works / is working** on Saturdays.'
2 'Are Andy and Peter in the garden?'
'No, they **play / are playing** a computer game.'
3 'Is Teresa at school now?'
'No, school **finishes / is finishing** at four o'clock.'
4 'Are Mum and Dad at home?'
'Yes, they **pack / are packing** their suitcases.'
5 'Are you a good student?'
'Yes, I often **get / am getting** good marks.'

8 Write the correct form of the verbs: present simple or present continuous.

We (**1**) ...live... (**live**) in Canada. My dad's a farmer. He (**2**) .... (**work**) twelve hours every day. In the winter, it often (**3**) .... (**snow**) . It's cold today, but it (**4**) .... (**not snow**). I (**5**) .... (**wear**) a big coat and gloves because I (**6**) .... (**help**) my dad outside. We (**7**) .... (**move**) the animals into a new field. My mum is in the house. She (**8**) .... (**make**) lunch.

Vocabulary

9 Look at the examples from the text. Make nouns for jobs from the verbs in the box.

verb		noun
build	+ er	builder
drive (a truck)	+ er	(a truck) driver

| farm | report | sing | teach | work | wait |

See Vocabulary Explorer: Page 101

10 What's the job? Read the information and decide.

This person works with animals. This person doesn't wear a uniform. This person works outside and uses a tractor.

11 Choose a job from *Vocabulary Explorer: Page 101*. Write sentences like those in Exercise 10. Then work in pairs and exchange your sentences. What's the job?

Study skills

Using a dictionary (2)

cold *adj* at a low temperature
n an illness, an infection of the nose and throat

farm *n* an area of land where you grow food or keep animals
v to work and earn money growing food or keeping animals

1 Look at the dictionary entries. What do *adj*, *n* and *v* mean?

2 Are the underlined words *adjectives, nouns* or *verbs?* Check in your dictionary.
   1 It's <u>raining</u> again!
   2 Look at the <u>rain</u>.
   3 Your car is <u>clean</u>!
   4 It often <u>snows</u> here.

Halloween
Magic Show

25-31 October
Royal Theatre

a

Horror Film
Festival

26 Oct - 5 Nov
Orion Multicinemas

b

Halloween
Fair

21-31 October
Town Hall

c

Reading and listening

1 2.5 **Read and listen to the dialogue. Choose the correct poster (a, b or c).**

Kate:	Hi, is Lewis there, please?
Lewis's dad:	No, I'm sorry. He's out. Who's calling?
Kate:	It's Kate.
Lewis's dad:	Oh hello, Kate. Do you want to leave a message?
Kate:	Yes, please.
Lewis's dad:	OK, hang on. I'm just looking for a pen. OK.
Kate:	Well, Judy and I are at the Town Hall, and we're waiting for Lewis. The Halloween Fair closes at half past two.
Lewis's dad:	OK. Can you repeat the time?
Kate:	Half past two.
Lewis's dad:	OK, that's Kate and Judy, Halloween Fair, half past two.
Kate:	Yes, that's right.
Lewis's dad:	Actually, Kate, I think Lewis is with Adam. Why don't you phone Adam's house?
Kate:	Oh thanks, that's a good idea.
Lewis's dad:	Bye!
Kate:	Bye.

2 Read the message Lewis's dad wrote. Correct the mistakes.

> Lewis – Judy phoned. She and Kate are going to a Halloween party. It starts at 2.30.
>
> Dad

3 2.6 **Listen to the phone calls and complete the messages.**

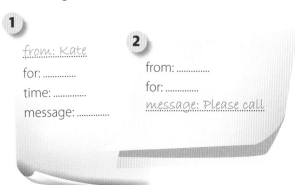

1

from: Kate
for: ....
time: ....
message: ....

2

from: ....
for: ....
message: Please call

4 2.7 **Listen and repeat the *Useful expressions*. Focus on your intonation.**

USEFUL EXPRESSIONS

Hello. / Hi.	Do you want to leave a message?
Is Kate there?	
No, I'm sorry.	Can I leave a message?
Yes, just a moment.	Can you repeat that?
Who's calling?	Bye.
It's Adam.	

Speaking

5 Work in pairs. Practise giving and taking phone messages. Use the *Useful expressions*. Take turns.

A: Choose a poster (a, b or c) from the opposite page. You are at the event. You are waiting for your friend. Phone your friend's house.

B: Answer the phone. Take a message for your brother/sister.

e.g. A: *Hello, is … there?*
B: *No, I'm sorry. This is his/her …*

Pronunciation: syllable stress

6 2.8 **Listen and repeat the words in Groups 1 and 2. Notice which syllable is stressed.**

1 ● ●   **2 ● ●**

1	2
autumn	arrive
builder	begin
London	behind
measure	correct
mobile	guitar
pilot	mistake
tractor	perform
weather	repeat

7 2.9 **Say each word. Which syllable is stressed? Then listen, check and repeat.**

doctor	message	moment
monsoon	police	travel

Writing: describing a friend

1 Read and match the description with the correct photo.

2 Write a description of the second photo. Use this information.

This / Linda
live / next door
love / Robbie Williams
listen to his records / every day
In this photo, play / her guitar
In summer / practise outside

3 Find or take a photo of a friend and write a description. Give information about his/her hobbies and what he/she is doing in the photo.

`My Friends` site
Friendbook
sitemap   registration   login
search

Home   About us   Gallery   Products   Contact

My best friend

This is my best friend Linda. She lives in my street. She loves music and she plays the piano, the guitar and the violin. She goes to music classes every day after school. In this photo, she's playing her guitar in the living room. She's practising for the school concert. She spends hours practising. She's a bit crazy – she calls her guitar Robbie because she likes Robbie Williams.

Reading

1 What do you think the weather is like in Canada?

> cold   hot   icy   stormy   sunny

2 🔊 2.10 **Read the text and check your answers to Exercise 1.**

3 **Read the text again and answer the questions.**

1 Which country has got a border with Canada?
2 Which part of Canada do most Canadians live in?
3 What's the weather like in the north of Canada in summer?
4 Which wild animals can you see in Canada?
5 How many National Parks are there in Canada?
6 What free-time activities can you do in the National Parks?

Culture

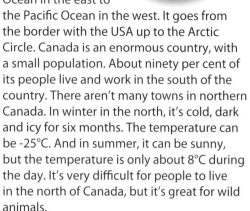

Canada

Canada stretches from the Atlantic Ocean in the east to the Pacific Ocean in the west. It goes from the border with the USA up to the Arctic Circle. Canada is an enormous country, with a small population. About ninety per cent of its people live and work in the south of the country. There aren't many towns in northern Canada. In winter in the north, it's cold, dark and icy for six months. The temperature can be -25°C. And in summer, it can be sunny, but the temperature is only about 8°C during the day. It's very difficult for people to live in the north of Canada, but it's great for wild animals.

You can see animals like wolves and moose. There are polar bears and grizzly bears too. They can be dangerous, especially when they have young bear cubs. Wolves don't like going near people, but moose sometimes go into small towns. These animals often live in the National Park areas. There are nearly forty National Parks in Canada. You can go walking, fishing and skiing in the National Parks. But watch out for the bears!

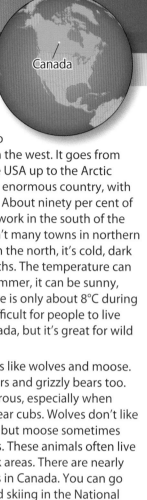

Listening

4 🔊 2.11 **Listen to a radio programme about a family that lives close to one of the Canadian National Parks. Choose the correct option.**

1 The Spencer family is Canadian / English.

2 The Spencers live in Jasper / near Jasper.

3 Alison teaches skiing / swimming.

4 Diane is Alison's daughter / mum.

5 Charlie drives a school bus / a snow sled.

5 🔊 2.11 **Listen again and choose the correct name.**

1 Diane / Alison / Charlie wants to be a teacher.

2 Diane / Alison / Charlie is a shop assistant.

3 Diane / Alison / Charlie has two jobs.

4 Diane / Alison / Charlie sells clothes.

5 Diane / Alison / Charlie makes ice sculptures.

Project

Keep a weather diary for a week. Write the temperature and the weather each day.

Chemistry and English
Crystals

1 Work in pairs. Do you know what snow, salt and diamonds have got in common?

2 Read the text and find the answer.

What are crystals?
Crystals are solid materials. They are usually very small and they can have different shapes.

Where can I see crystals?
You can see crystals in your kitchen – salt is a crystal. And you can see crystals in winter – ice is solid water and snow is made of ice crystals. And people wear crystals too. Diamonds are crystals.

How do crystals form?
Crystals form in different ways. For example, ice crystals form when the temperature goes below 0°C. At 0°C, water changes from a liquid to a solid. In winter, this happens inside clouds and tiny ice crystals form. The crystals fall to the ground – snowflakes! Each one is a different shape and size.

3 Look at the photos. What exactly can you see?

Review Units 1 and 2

Vocabulary

1 Write the interests.

1 cats, bears, fish   a ....
2 pop, hip hop, classical   m ....
3 books, comics   r ....
4 football, tennis   s ....
5 clothes, bags, shoes   f ....

1 mark per item: …/5 marks

2 Write the activities.

1 I like p .... the violin.
2 My best friend loves t .... photos.
3 My brother loves w .... TV.
4 I don't like c .... very much, so I haven't got a bike.
5 I like art at school. I like p ....

1 mark per item: …/5 marks

3 Complete the sentences with words about performances.

1 Actors wear .... on their faces.
2 Animals often perform in a ....
3 I'm acting in a .... at school.
4 My friend plays the drums in a rock ....
5 I love carnivals. This year I'm wearing a fantastic ....

1 mark per item: …/5 marks

4 Write the weather words.

1 ....   4 ....
2 ....   5 ....
3 ....

1 mark per item: …/5 marks

5 Write the jobs.

1 He works in a shop.
2 She works on your teeth.
3 He works in a restaurant.
4 She works with students.
5 He flies a plane.

1 mark per item: …/5 marks

Grammar

6 Write sentences and questions with the present simple.

1 She / live / in America.
2 I / not study / Italian.
3 you / work / with animals?
4 he / teach / maths?
5 She / not like / hip hop.

1 mark per item: …/5 marks

7 Write the sentences using the adverbs of frequency.

1 I eat meat. (**never**)
2 We're happy. (**always**)
3 She doesn't wear make up. (**usually**)
4 They aren't at home. (**often**)
5 We go to the cinema on Fridays. (**sometimes**)

1 mark per item: …/5 marks

8 Complete the questions and answers.

1 .... you reading this book? Yes, ...
2 .... Kate watching TV? No, ...
3 .... your friends coming? Yes, ...
4 .... you wearing make up? No, ...
5 .... it raining outside? Yes, ...

1 mark per item: …/5 marks

9 Complete the sentences with the present simple or present continuous.

1 On Saturdays, we .... shopping. (**go**)
2 Oh no! It .... outside again. (**snow**)
3 Paula usually .... to school. (**walk**)
4 David .... to the teacher. He's asleep! (**not / listen**)
5 The number 56 bus .... to the city centre. (**not / go**)

1 mark per item: …/5 marks

10 Complete the sentences.

1 My mum is .... nurse.
2 'It's hot!' 'Well, take .... your jacket!'
3 My brother drives a truck. He's a truck ....
4 I go to the pool every day. I love ....
5 How .... do you go to the cinema?

1 mark per item: …/5 marks

Communicate

11 Complete the dialogue with these words.

> like   love   this   where   why

Damian: Hi, Jill! (**1**) .... is my friend, Neil.
Jill: Hi, Neil. Do you (**2**) .... skateboarding?
Neil: Yes, I (**3**) .... it! It's great.
Jill: (**4**) .... don't you join our club?
Neil: (**5**) .... do you meet?
Jill: At the skate park, every evening.
Neil: OK!

2 marks per item: …/10 marks

12 Choose the correct response.

1 Why don't we go for a burger?
  a OK, great idea.
  b Yes, I do.
  c No, I don't.

2 I'm bored.
  a Are you bored?
  b Let's watch a film.
  c Good idea! Me too!

3 How about a game of tennis?
  a No thanks, I don't like tennis.
  b Yes, it does.
  c Yes, I do.

4 Hello, can I leave a message for Sally?
  a No, I'm sorry. She's out.
  b No, this isn't Sally.
  c Yes, of course.

5 Who's calling?
  a I am me.
  b I'm Holly.
  c It's Holly.

2 marks per item: …/10 marks

13 Find the two words in each group with the stress on the first syllable.

1 moment   message   begin
2 guitar   travel   Sunday
3 teacher   scary   repeat
4 police   pilot   doctor
5 sunny   arrive   raining

2 marks per item: …/10 marks

14 Complete the phone conversation with the sentences.

> Can you repeat that?
> No, I'm sorry. He's out.
> Oh hello, Jill. Do you want to leave a message?
> Bye, Jill.
> OK.

Jill: Hi, is Neil there, please?
Neil's mum: (**1**) ....
Jill: Oh. Well, it's Jill here.
Neil's mum: (**2**) ....
Jill: Yes, please. We're all waiting at the café in Brown Street.
Neil's mum: (**3**) ....
Jill: Yes, we're at the café in Brown Street.
Neil's mum: (**4**) ....
Jill: Thanks very much.
Neil's mum: (**5**) ....
Jill: Bye.

2 marks per item: …/10 marks

15 Complete the website profile with these words.

> 'm   a   and   are   do   going   my
> sometimes   the   to

Hi! My name's Jill. I go (**1**) .... Ashford School. My favourite subjects (**2**) .... music and art. In my free time, I like (**3**) .... to concerts. I play (**4**) .... piano and the guitar. In this photo, I (**5**) .... playing my guitar. My ambition is to be (**6**) .... professional musician. What are (**7**) .... weak points? Well, I (**8**) .... fight with my little sister. (**9**) .... you like my profile? Why don't you click on my photo (**10**) .... write to me?

1 mark per item: …/10 marks

Total: …/100

I can...

I can make suggestions.
I can talk about likes and dislikes.
I can make phone calls.
I can leave phone messages.

A questionnaire

Reading

1 Read the questionnaire and answer the questions.

Tell us about yourself!

Name: Matt Hughes **Age: 25**

Where are you from?
Originally, I'm from New Zealand.

Where are you living now?
Right now, I'm living in London.

What's the weather like today?
It's raining!

Where do you work?
I work in a restaurant. I'm a chef.

How many people are there where you work?
There are about ten people in the kitchen.

How old are the people there?
All ages. From 19 to 50.

How old is the restaurant?
It's new, actually. About six months old.

Do you like your job?
Yes. It's hard work. But I like it.

What do you do when you finish work for the day?
I go home and sleep! I work in the evenings, so it's late when I finish.

What is your favourite free-time activity?
I like going to the cinema.

How often do you go to the cinema?
I sometimes go to the cinema at weekends.

Can you play any musical instruments?
No, but I love singing!

Are you in a band?
No! I sing in the bathroom!

How often do you go out with friends?
I usually see my friends on Saturday nights.

Finally … what do you want to do now?
Well, right now , I want to have some lunch. Then I want to listen to some music and check my emails.

Thanks for answering my questions!
My pleasure!

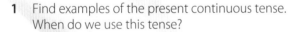

1 Find examples of the present continuous tense. When do we use this tense?
2 What tense does the writer use for the other questions? Why?
3 How does the writer ask questions? Make a list.

   e.g. *Where … ?*
   What's … ?
   Are you … ?
   How many … ?

2 **Make more questions using these words. What other questions can you think of?**

1 you / play / any musical instruments?
2 What / be / your full name?
3 How old / be / you?
4 What / you / wear / to school?
5 What / you / wear / today?
6 be / the sun / shine / now?

Project

Write your own questionnaire.

• Choose who you want to ask
• Write your questions for that person
• Ask your questions (you can do this by telephone or email)
• Write down their answers quickly
• Write the questions and answers together carefully
• Add a photograph or a drawing of the person to your questionnaire

Words and pictures

3

> **Grammar**

Learn about the past simple, and question words.

> **Vocabulary**

Learn words for mass media, films, and television programmes.

> **Skills**

Read about the history of writing, Hollywood films, and American icons.

Listen to a conversation about films.

Write a blog entry.

> **Communicate**

Express and ask for opinions, and agree and disagree.

1 Work in pairs. What can you see in the photo?

2 Work with a new partner and compare your ideas.

3 ◉ 3.1 Listen to a radio news programme. What is the main news story?

   a the European Union

   b the economy

   c the weather

4 What kind of news do you find from these things? Discuss these ways with your partner.

> blogs   email   the Internet   podcasts
> text   messages   TV

See Vocabulary Explorer: Page 102

33

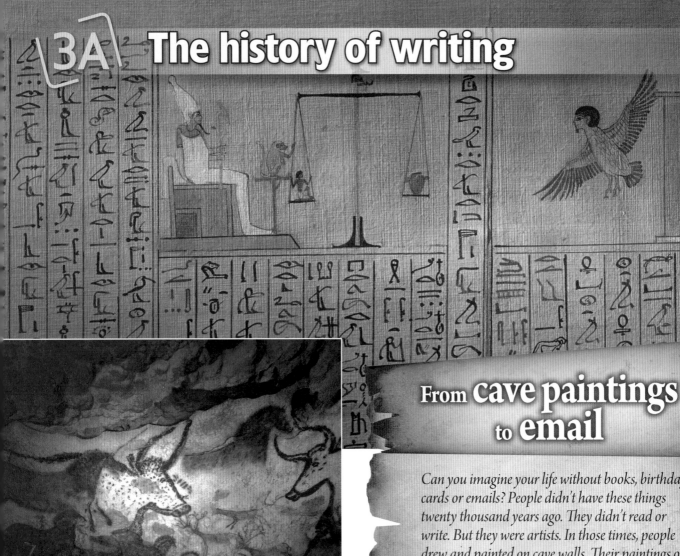

From cave paintings to email

Can you imagine your life without books, birthday cards or emails? People didn't have these things twenty thousand years ago. They didn't read or write. But they were artists. In those times, people drew and painted on cave walls. Their paintings of animals and people were the first recorded stories.

About five thousand years ago, the Egyptians also painted on walls. They painted hieroglyphs – small pictures – on the walls of the pyramids. Each picture represented one word.

A thousand years later, people in Samaria (modern-day Iraq) invented cuneiform – a new system of symbols. Each symbol represented one sound. Different combinations of symbols made different words. It was a good system, but it wasn't fast. It took a long time to write by hand. Then in 1453, a man called Gutenberg made a machine to print words on paper. Suddenly, it was possible to make many copies of a book quickly. For the first time, ordinary people began to read. About four hundred years ago, the first newspapers appeared. Ordinary people also began to send letters with personal news to their family and friends.

Finally, about twenty years ago, computers became popular. Now we use email and the Internet to write to our friends – without printing or paper.

Vocabulary

1 Complete the sentences with the words in the box.

e.g. My favourite _book_ is *Treasure Island*.

> book   DVDs   magazine
> newspaper   radio   television

1 My dad reads the .... every morning.
2 My mum listens to the .... in the car.
3 My favourite .... programme is *The X Factor*.
4 At home, we watch .... with English subtitles.
5 I buy a computer .... every month.

See Vocabulary Explorer: Page 102

2 Work in pairs. Ask and answer questions about some of the things in Exercise 1.

e.g. A: *What's your favourite book / television programme / magazine?*

B: *My favourite…*

Reading and listening

3 ◯ 3.2 What can you see in the pictures? Read and listen to the text and check your answers.

4 Read the text again and complete the time line.

- The first newspapers appeared.
- Gutenberg invented a printing machine.
- The Egyptians painted pictures called hieroglyphs.
- The Samarians wrote with the cuneiform system.

T I M E L I N E	20,000 years ago	People made cave paintings.
	5,000 years ago	....
	4,000 years ago	....
	550 years ago	....
	400 years ago	....
	20 years ago	We started using email.

Grammar: past simple *be*

5 Look at the example. Find five more sentences in the text with the past simple of *be*.

But they were artists.

6 Complete the table with the words in the box.

was   wasn't   were   weren't

Affirmative	
I/He/She/It	**(1)** .... an artist.
You/We/They	**(2)** .... artists.
Negative	
I/He/She/It	**(3)** .... fast.
You/We/They	**(4)** .... in Egypt.

See Grammar Explorer: Page 123

7 Complete the sentences with the past simple form of *be*.

e.g. Gutenberg's printing machine .was. quick.

1 The pharaohs .... Egyptian kings.
2 The cuneiform system .... (not) fast.

Grammar: past simple regular and irregular verbs

8 Complete the table with the words in the box.

began   didn't read   painted

Affirmative		
Regular	The Egyptians	**(1)** .... hieroglyphs.
Irregular	Ordinary people	**(2)** .... to read.
Negative	They	**(3)** .... or write.

See Grammar Explorer: Page 124

9 Find the regular past simple verbs and circle the irregular ones in the text.

10 Complete the sentences with the past simple forms of the verbs.

e.g. We .saw. a great film at the cinema last weekend. (**see**)

1 We .... *The Hobbit* at school last year. (**read**)
2 Thirty years ago my grandparents .... a black and white TV. (**have**)
3 I .... television yesterday evening – I did my homework. (**not watch**)
4 I .... to write when I .... five years old. (**learn / be**)
5 When we .... little, we .... a letter to Santa Claus every Christmas. (**be / write**)

11 Complete the email with the correct forms of the verbs in the box.

be   find   not like   look for   think   watch

Hi Tim,

Thanks for your email about the TV programme last night. I **(1)** .... it with my brother. It **(2)** .... really interesting! My brother **(3)** .... the part about the snakes! I **(4)** .... it was great. After the programme, we **(5)** .... information on the Internet. We **(6)** .... two great websites: www.snake.pt and www. megasnake.edu.

See you,

Phil

Working with words

12 Look at the example. Then replace the underlined words with the expressions in the box.

e.g. My grandfather sent this letter 2 years ago.
.four weeks.

1 We went to Norway in January.
2 I bought this magazine last weekend.

April   four weeks   month
night   Saturday   September
three months   five days

Fast finishers

Find four pairs of verbs. Write a sentence with each verb in the past simple.

end   read   send   begin   speak
write   listen   receive

2016 from English Explorer 2 - Helen Stephenson Cengage

Blockbusters – the big, big movies

Steven Spielberg directed his first film, *Firelight*, in 1964. He was sixteen. It was a science fiction film. Spielberg showed the film at a cinema in his hometown. Five hundred people bought tickets. *Jaws* was Spielberg's fifth film. It broke cinema records in 1975 – it made over $7 million in one weekend. People enjoyed frightening films! In total, *Jaws* made $260 million in the USA and $470 million around the world. It was the first 'blockbuster' film. The next enormously successful film was *Star Wars*. Millions of people went to see it on its first night, in 1977. The film used amazing special effects. Special effects were also important in the top blockbuster film of all time – *Titanic*. This film made $1.8 billion, and it won 11 Oscars. Leonardo DiCaprio and Kate Winslet starred in the film. Some people went to see *Titanic* more than ten times!

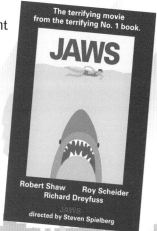

The terrifying movie from the terrifying No. 1 book.

JAWS

Robert Shaw   Roy Scheider
Richard Dreyfuss

JAWS
directed by Steven Spielberg

Blockbuster Quiz – How much do you know about the top ten movies of all time?

1 When did the Titanic sink?
2 Who were Batman's enemies in *The Dark Knight*?
3 What did the Jedi knights use in fights in *Star Wars*?
4 Who did the Dragon fall in love with in *Shrek*?
5 Where did E.T. come from?
6 In *Pirates of the Caribbean*, what was Captain Sparrow's first name?
7 Why did Peter Parker turn into Spiderman?
8 Were the Hobbits happy at the end of *Lord of the Rings*?
9 How did the scientists create the dinosaurs in *Jurassic Park*?
10 Did Harry Potter live with his parents?

KEY
1 in 1912   2 the Joker and Two-Face   3 laser sabres   4 Donkey   5 Space   6 Jack   7 A spider bit him.
8 Yes, because they went home.   9 They cloned them.   10 No, he lived with his aunt and uncle.

9–10 Well done! You're an expert!
5–8 Not bad – maybe you prefer TV.
0–4 Oh dear. Don't you like the movies?

Vocabulary

1 Work in pairs. Match the film titles (1–6) with the film types (a–f). Then add another film to each group.

1	*Indiana Jones*	a	action
2	*The Lord of the Rings*	b	cartoon
3	*Mamma Mia*	c	fantasy
4	*Shrek*	d	musical
5	*The Matrix*	e	romance
6	*Titanic*	f	science fiction

See Vocabulary Explorer: Page 103

2 Work in pairs. What's your favourite film? Tell your partner about it.

Reading and listening

3 3.3 **Read and listen to the text. What are blockbusters?**

a Hollywood film stars
b successful films
c film directors

4 **Read the text again. Are the sentences true or false?**

1 Jaws made $7 million in one weekend.
2 *Star Wars* was the first blockbuster film.
3 *Titanic* won two Oscars.

5 **Work in pairs. Answer the questions in the Blockbuster Quiz. Then check your answers in the key.**

Grammar: past simple question forms

6 Complete the table with *was, wasn't, were* and *weren't*.

Questions		
(1)	*Titanic*	successful?
(2)	the Hobbits	happy?
Short answers		
Yes,/No,	it	was./**(3)** ....
Yes,/No,	they	were./**(4)** ....

See Grammar Explorer: Page 124

7 Write questions with the past simple of *be* and these words. Then work in pairs. Ask and answer the questions.

e.g. *Jaws* / frightening? <u>Was Jaws frightening?</u>

1 Spielberg's films / successful?
2 special effects / important?
3 the Joker / Batman's friend?
4 the Hobbits / human?
5 *Titanic* / a science fiction film?

8 Complete the table with words from the Blockbuster Quiz.

Questions with *did*		
(1)	Harry Potter **(2)** .... with his parents?	
Short answers		
Yes,	he	did.
No,	he	didn't.

See Grammar Explorer: Page 124

9 Complete the questions with the verbs in the box. Then look at the text and find the answers. Test your partner.

> direct   make   see   star   use

1 Did Steven Spielberg .... his first film in 1954?
2 Did *Jaws* .... $260 million in one weekend?
3 Did millions of people .... *Star Wars* on its first night?
4 Did *Titanic* .... special effects?
5 Did Kate Winslet .... in *Titanic*?

10 Complete the table with words from the quiz.

Questions with *Wh-* words		
(1) .... **(2)**	was were	Captain Sparrow's first name? Batman's enemies?
(3) .... **(4)** .... **(5)** .... **(6)** .... How many Oscars	did	the Titanic sink? E.T. come from? Peter Parker turn into Spiderman? the scientists create the dinosaurs? *Titanic* win?

Listening

11 🔊 3.4 **Listen to Paul and Anne talking about the film quiz. Choose the correct answers.**

1 Paul thought *Titanic* was
   a surprising.   **b** amazing.   **c** boring.
2 Anne thought *Star Wars* was
   a exciting.   **b** confusing.   **c** frightening.

Working with words

12 **Look at the examples. Then choose the correct adjectives.**

e.g. The film was confusing.
We were confused.

1 Action films are **exciting / excited**.
2 I was **surprising / surprised** when that film won an Oscar.
3 The special effects were **amazed / amazing**.
4 Was that programme **interesting / interested**?
5 Are you **boring / bored**? Let's go out.
6 I'm **tiring / tired** today.

See Grammar Explorer: Page 124

Study skills

Predicting

Follow these steps before you read or listen to English.

1 Look at the title. What do you know about the topic?
2 Look at the picture(s). What can you see?
3 Write ten words connected with the topic and picture(s).
4 Read or listen and look for your words.

Agreeing and disagreeing

Reading and listening

1 3.5 **Read and listen to the dialogue. Which programme do Adam, Lewis, Judy and Kate decide to watch?**

a *The Natural World* **b** *Prison Break* **c** *The X Factor*

Judy:	What's on TV tonight, Adam?
Adam:	Hey! Eight o'clock on BBC2 – *The Natural World*! That's a great programme.
Judy:	No way! I think it's really boring.
Adam:	Are you serious? I think it's brilliant!
Judy:	I prefer reality TV shows – they're interesting!
Lewis:	I agree. And the people on *The X Factor* are amazing.
Adam:	Kate, what's your opinion?
Katy:	I agree with Judy and Lewis. But *The X Factor* isn't on tonight.
Adam:	Well, *Prison Break* is on Channel 5. Do you like that?
Katy:	Yes, it's OK. I enjoy it, actually.
Judy:	Me too.
Adam:	What do you think of it, Lewis?
Lewis:	I don't mind it – it's OK.
Adam:	Do you want to watch it?
Lewis:	Yes, let's watch it.

2 Read the dialogue again and complete these ways of asking for opinions.

1 What's your ....?
2 Do you .... that?
3 What do you .... of it?

3 Complete the lists with expressions from the dialogue.

Agreeing	Disagreeing
I agree.	I don't agree.
....	....

4 3.6 **Listen and repeat the** *Useful expressions*. **Focus on your intonation.**

USEFUL EXPRESSIONS

What's your opinion?
Do you like comedies?
What do you think of this film?
I think it's great.
I don't mind it.
Me too.
I agree with Judy.
I don't agree with Adam.
No way!

Speaking

5 Write a list of six of your favourite TV programmes, films and books. Then work in groups. Talk to the people in your group and find out their opinions of the things on your list.

	Anna	Peter	Karen
Spiderman 3	boring	exciting	

Pronunciation: *-ed* endings

6 3.7 **Listen to these verbs and write them in the table. Repeat.**

developed   enjoyed   invented
liked   looked   painted
printed   represented   showed
starred   used   watched

/t/	/d/	/ɪd/
developed	enjoyed	invented

7 3.8 **Say each verb. Then listen, check and repeat.**

created   finished   helped
listened   lived   started

Writing: a blog entry

1 Read Lewis's blog entry. Answer the questions.

1 Where did he go?
2 Who did he go with?
3 Why did he go?
4 What did he do?
5 What were his opinions?

2 Find examples of *because* and *but* in the blog. Choose the correct word in the sentences.

1 Yesterday was interesting **because / but** it was very tiring.
2 I didn't watch the film **because / but** it was boring.
3 He gave me his pen **because / but** I didn't have one.
4 I saw her **but / because** she didn't see me.

3 Write a blog entry about a day in your recent past. Use the questions from Exercise 1 to help you plan your paragraph.

Last weekend was interesting! We went to a TV studio because my friend had tickets for *Who Wants To Be A Millionaire?* We were in the audience and we sat in the front row! It was a special celebrity programme. The questions were easy but the celebrities didn't know the answers! Anyway, it was a success because they made over €25,000 for Oxfam. At the end of the programme, the celebrities talked to the audience. I met an actor from *Prison Break*, but I didn't know what to say! It was amazing!

Culture

USA

Reading

1 Work in pairs. Look at the pictures of American icons. Do you know what they are?

2 3.9 **Read the text. Match the paragraphs (1–4) with four of the photos (a–f).**

3 Read the text again and put the events in the correct order.

  a Disney created Mickey Mouse.

  b France gave America the Statue of Liberty.

  c Hawaii became the 50th American state.

  d The American flag had thirteen stripes.

  e The Hollywood sign appeared.

1 The Hollywood sign is in Los Angeles, California. Each letter is 15 metres high. You can see the sign from many parts of the city. At first, the sign wasn't a symbol of the film industry. It was a 1923 advertisement for new houses in the area. But many people began to associate the sign with Hollywood films. These days, film stars sometimes pay for the repair of the sign.

2 Mickey Mouse was eighty years old in 2008. Walt Disney created Mickey Mouse in 1928 and he performed Mickey's voice on film until 1946. Mickey Mouse cartoons were very popular and eventually Mickey became the symbol of the Walt Disney Company.

3 The flag of the United States is red, white, and blue. The stars represent the states. The first flag of 1776 had thirteen stripes. These represented the thirteen original American colonies. Every time a new state joined the USA, the flag changed. The last change was in 1960 when Hawaii became the 50th state.

4 The Statue of Liberty is in the middle of New York City Harbour. It was a gift from France to the USA in 1886. It was a celebration of one hundred years of American Independence. In the past, people arrived in America by ship, not by plane. The Statue of Liberty was the first thing they saw. It represented a new life of freedom for many people.

Listening

4 🔊 3.10 **Listen to the story of one of the other two icons. Which one is it?**

5 🔊 3.10 **Listen again. Tick the places that are important in the story of this icon.**

France   Hamburg,
Germany   Hamburg,
New York   Mongolia
Texas

f

History and English
The New World

1 **Work in pairs. What do you know about the New World? Discuss these questions with your partner.**

1 What was the 'New World'?

2 Did the 15th century explorers travel by land or by sea?

3 When did Europeans first go to the American continent?

2 **Read the article and check your answers.**

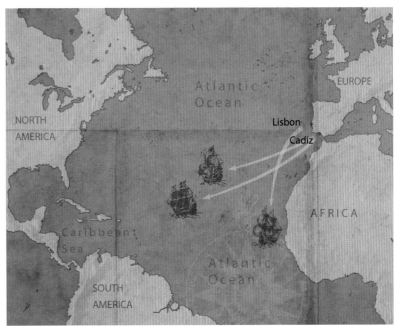

The end of the 15th century was an exciting period in European history. Powerful countries, especially Spain and Portugal, wanted to find new routes to countries in Asia. It took a long time to travel by land, but journeys by sea were fast. Spain and Portugal paid men like Christopher Columbus, Ferdinand Magellan and Vasco da Gama to look for new sea routes. Columbus and Magellan sailed west. Vasco de Gama sailed east. They all discovered places and people the Europeans didn't know about. Columbus's first voyage was in 1492. He arrived on a Caribbean island, but he thought it was Asia. Ten years later, Amerigo Vespucci realised that Columbus's discovery was a different continent – America. It was a 'New World' for Europe.

3 **Why do you think European countries wanted to find quick routes to Asia?**

Project

Work in pairs. Choose two symbols of your country and find out about their history. Find a photo and write a paragraph about each symbol.

Ahmed bin Majid

1 Read the article about Ahmed bin Majid below and correct the information in these sentences.

1 We are sure when he was born.
2 We know exactly where he lived.
3 He knew how to sail ships before he was 17.
4 People called him the *Lion of the Sea* because he was a good student.
5 All of his books are about poetry.
6 We are sure of the date of his death.
7 A Portuguese sailor travelled to India before seeing bin Majid's map.
8 People named a hotel after him.

1421

1500

Ahmed bin Majid

He was born in 1421 (some people say in 1430) in Julphar (now called Ras Al Khaimah in the United Arab Emirates). Some historians say that he later lived in Al Ghob, and archaeologists often dig in the area to try to find his home.

At the age of 17, he learned how to sail ships. He was interested in astronomy and geography and he studied the stars, the moon, and the weather – particularly the wind. He followed the stars when he sailed at night and he didn't get lost.

He spent 50 years at sea! People called him the *Lion of the Sea* because he was so brave.

He wrote over 40 books, including many poems and lots of very useful information to help sailors get to the coasts of India and East Africa safely.

Ahmed bin Majid's work helped to create a map and the Portuguese sailor, Vasco da Gama, used it to find his way between Europe and India. Thanks to Ahmed bin Majid, ships could sail safely around Africa to where they wanted to go.

Ahmed bin Majid died sometime around 1500.

There is a school named after him in Muscat, Oman. We remember him as a great Arab sailor and explorer.

2 Complete the sentences with the words in the box.

was	wanted	spent	found
knew	wrote		

1 Years ago, travelling by ship .... very dangerous.
2 He .... how to sail at night and not get lost.
3 He .... long periods of time at sea.
4 Ahmed bin Majid .... books and drew maps for other sailors to use.
5 Vasco da Gama used Majid's maps and .... a way from Europe to the East.
6 Sailors sailed to where they .... to go.

Biographies

4

> Grammar

Learn about the past continuous
and the past simple.

> Vocabulary

Learn words for life events, and for
describing a person's appearance.

> Skills

Read about a Maasai boy from Kenya,
pirates, and Australian heroes.

Listen to a description of famous criminals.

Write a biography.

> Communicate

Make and accept apologies,
and tell stories.

1 Work in pairs. What can you see
in the photo?

2 4.1 **Listen. Who is the
conversation about?**

a a singer
b a writer
c a painter

3 **Think of three famous people
you admire. Can you describe
their appearance? What do they
do? Why do you admire them?**

See Vocabulary Explorer: Page 105

4 **Work in pairs. Tell your partner
about your heroes.**

43

My name is Joseph Lekuton. I was born in Kenya and I grew up there. I'm a Maasai. Maasai people are nomads. They move from place to place with their animals. When I was growing up, only one child from each Maasai family went to school – that was me. I lived at school and I went home in the holidays.

One holiday, when I was 14, I went to help my brothers. They were travelling with my family's cows. During the night, lions attacked the cows. The next morning, we saw the lions. They were eating a dead cow. The young lions weren't moving.

A big male lion was looking at me. His tail was hitting the ground, slowly and repeatedly. I was shaking with fear. Suddenly, the lion gave a loud roar. I ran home. I was happy to go back to school.

Four years later, I left school. First, I passed an exam and then I went to university in the USA. Once more, I was afraid. But I graduated from university. After that, I got a job as a teacher. Then I returned to Kenya and my people. I became a politician and now I work in the Kenyan government.

Reading and listening

1   Work in pairs. Look at the photos and discuss the questions.

   1   Where do you think the man is from?

   2   What do lions eat?

2   4.2 **Read and listen to the story. Answer the questions.**

   1   Who is the story about?

   2   What is a Maasai?

   3   Where did he study?

   4   What is his job now?

3   **Read the story again and answer the questions.**

   1   Where did Joseph go in the school holidays?

   2   What happened in the night?

   3   What did they see in the morning?

   4   What did Joseph do?

Vocabulary

4   Complete the life events with the verbs in the box.

> became   got   graduated   grew
> left   passed   was   went

a   .... an exam

b   .... from university

c   .... a job

d   .... up

e   .... school

f   .... a politician

g   .... to university

h   .... born

See Vocabulary Explorer: Page 104

5   **Put the events in Exercise 4 in the correct order. Check the order in the story.**

Grammar: past continuous

6 Complete the sentences from the story.

1   They *was travelling* .... with my family's cows.
2   The young lions *moving* ....
3   A big male lion .... at me.
4   I .... with fear.

7 Complete the tables with *was, wasn't, were* and *weren't*.

Affirmative	
I/He/She/It You/We/They	**(1)** *was* growing up. **(2)** *were* travelling.
Negative	
I/He/She/It You/We/They	**(3)** *wasn't* shaking. **(4)** *weren't* moving.

Questions		
(5) *was* **(6)** *were*	I/he/she/it you/we/they	looking at the lion?
Short answers		
Yes,	I/he/she/it you/we/they	**(7)** *was* were.
No,	I/he/she/it you/we/they	wasn't. **(8)** *weren't*.

> Remember the spelling changes with some verbs: *move – moving, travel – travelling*.

See Grammar Explorer: Page 124

8 Find the past continuous verbs in the story. How many are there?

9 Complete the story with the past continuous form of the verbs.

> eat   make   move   run   shake   ~~snore~~

Last summer, we went camping in the mountains. During the night, I woke up many times. First, I woke up at midnight. My brothers **(1)** *were snoring*. Suddenly, we all woke up at 4 a.m. An animal **(2)** *were moving* around outside the tent! It **(3)** *was running* a strange noise. We lay quietly, but we **(4)** *were shake* with fear! Then the noise stopped. My dad looked outside. A bear **(5)** *was moving* to the woods. It **(6)** *was making* a big bar of chocolate – our chocolate! After that, we didn't sleep. We were afraid! The next morning, we packed the car and drove home.

10 Work in pairs. Look at the picture from last Sunday morning. Then cover the picture. Ask and answer questions. Take turns.

e.g. A: *What was the man doing?*
   B: *The man was . . .*

5 August 11:22

> ~~the man~~   the boy   the dog   the girls
> the baby   the shark   the woman

11 Write five times in the past and what you were doing. Then work in pairs. Take turns.

   A: Say a time.
   B: Guess what A was doing. You can only have four guesses!

e.g. A: *Five o'clock yesterday.*
   B: *Were you doing your homework?*
   A: *No, I wasn't.*

Working with words

12 Play a memory game and test your partner. Read the story in Exercise 9 from the beginning. Pause after each expression below. Can your partner remember the rest of the sentence?

During the night,	Then
First,	After that,
Suddenly,	The next morning,

Fast finishers

Which is the odd one out in each list. Why? Then write more lists for a partner.

1 exam	graduate	nomad	school
2 bear	cow	hunter	lion
3 afraid	attack	happy	loud
4 move	noise	run	walk

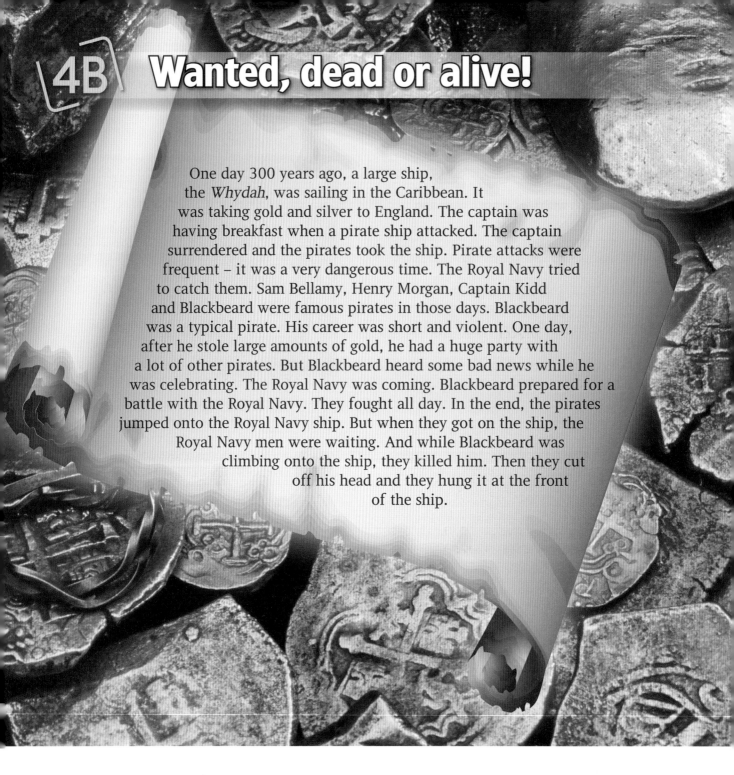

One day 300 years ago, a large ship, the *Whydah*, was sailing in the Caribbean. It was taking gold and silver to England. The captain was having breakfast when a pirate ship attacked. The captain surrendered and the pirates took the ship. Pirate attacks were frequent – it was a very dangerous time. The Royal Navy tried to catch them. Sam Bellamy, Henry Morgan, Captain Kidd and Blackbeard were famous pirates in those days. Blackbeard was a typical pirate. His career was short and violent. One day, after he stole large amounts of gold, he had a huge party with a lot of other pirates. But Blackbeard heard some bad news while he was celebrating. The Royal Navy was coming. Blackbeard prepared for a battle with the Royal Navy. They fought all day. In the end, the pirates jumped onto the Royal Navy ship. But when they got on the ship, the Royal Navy men were waiting. And while Blackbeard was climbing onto the ship, they killed him. Then they cut off his head and they hung it at the front of the ship.

Reading and listening

1 Work in pairs. What do you know about pirates? How many words can you write about them in two minutes?

2 The following words are all in the text. Do you know their meanings? Check in a dictionary if necessary.

> surrendered   Royal Navy   catch   career   hung

3 ○ 4.3 **Read and listen to the article. Choose the best title (a, b or c).**

a The pirate ship *Whydah*

b Life in the Royal Navy

c Pirates in the 18th century

Grammar: past simple and past continuous

4 **Complete the sentences from the text.**

1 The captain was having breakfast when …

2 Blackbeard heard some bad news while …

3 When they got on the ship, …

4 While Blackbeard was climbing onto the ship, …

5 **Match the sentence patterns with the sentences in Exercise 4.**

a *when* + past simple, past continuous

b *while* + past continuous, past simple

c past continuous + *when* + past simple

d past simple + *while* + past continuous

See Grammar Explorer: Page 125

6 Complete the sentences with the past simple or past continuous form of the verbs.

e.g. The ship _was sailing_ (sail) to England when Blackbeard _attacked_ (attack) it.

1 The pirates _celebrate_ (**celebrate**) when the Royal Navy _arrived_ (**arrive**).

2 While the men _have ing_ (**have**) a party, the pirates _attacked_ (**attack**).

3 The lion _killing_ (**kill**) a cow while we _sleeping_ (**sleep**). _killed_.

4 When he _got_ (**get**) to the camp, his brother _waiting_ (**wait**).

5 We _eating_ (**eat**) our lunch when we _hear_ (**hear**) the news.

7 Complete the email with the correct form of the verbs in the box.

> chase   crash   drive   flash
> get   see   show   ~~wait~~

Hi Jill,

It was great to see you yesterday. While we (**1**) _were waiting_ for the bus, we (**2**) _saw_ a big police chase! It was very dramatic. Three police cars (**3**) _were chasing_ a big black car. Their blue lights (**4**) _flashed_ and the sirens were going! One police car (**5**) _crash_ into the black car while it (**6**) _raced_ across the park. When we (**7**) _show_ home, they (**8**) _got_ the chase on the TV news!

See you! Robbie

Vocabulary

8 Look at the posters of wanted criminals (a–e). Match the words in the box with the criminals.

> a beard   black hair   blue eyes   brown eyes
> curly hair   fair hair   long hair   a moustache
> old   short hair   wavy hair   young

See Vocabulary Explorer: **Page 105**

Listening

9 4.4 **Listen to the descriptions of the criminals. Match the descriptions (1–5) with the posters (a–e) in Exercise 8.**

1 Blackbeard

2 Billy the Kid

3 Bonnie

4 Clyde

5 The Bandit Queen

10 Work in pairs. Look at the posters. Ask and answer questions about the criminals.

e.g. A: *What did Blackbeard look like?*

B: *He had ... He wore ...*

11 Play a memory game with your partner. Close your books. Ask and answer questions about the criminals. Begin your questions with *Did*.

e.g. A: *Did Blackbeard have a moustache?*

B: *Yes, he did.*

Study skills

New words

1 When there are new words in a text, follow these steps.

1 Look at the whole sentence. Can you guess the meaning of the word?

2 Decide if the word is a noun, a verb or an adjective. Can you think of other words for the new word?

3 Is the word an important word in the text? Look it up in your dictionary.

2 Guess the meanings of the underlined words. Then check in your dictionary.

1 The Bandit Queen wore silver <u>bracelets</u> on her arm.

2 Pirates often kept their gold and silver <u>treasure</u> in a large box.

3 Bonnie and Clyde stole thousands of dollars in bank <u>robberies</u>.

4 Some pirates wore a black <u>patch</u> over one eye.

5 Billy the Kid wasn't his real name – it was the <u>nickname</u> of Henry McCarty.

Apologising

Reading and listening

1 ○ 4.5 **Read and listen to the dialogue. What did Lewis forget?**

Kate: Good morning, Lewis! Have you got my Spanish book?

Lewis: Oh no!

Kate: What do you mean, 'Oh no'?

Lewis: I think I left it … on the kitchen table! I was hurrying because I was late.

Kate: But I've got a Spanish lesson this afternoon!

Lewis: I'm sorry. I'm very sorry!

Kate: Well, it doesn't matter. I can share with Judy.

Judy: No, you can't. I don't do Spanish, remember! I do French.

Lewis: I'm really sorry, Kate.

Kate: Never mind. Can you bring it at lunchtime?

Lewis: Yes, OK. I usually go home for lunch. I'm sorry!

Kate: Don't worry, it's all right. See you later!

Judy: Lewis, what's the matter? You look strange.

Lewis: Well, I don't think Kate's book is at home. I think I left it on the bus!

Judy: Oh, Lewis! You lost it!

2 ○ 4.6 **Listen and repeat the *Useful expressions*. Focus on your intonation.**

USEFUL EXPRESSIONS

I'm very sorry.
It doesn't matter.
Never mind.
Don't worry.
It's all right.

3 **Complete the dialogues with the verbs in the correct tense. Then work in pairs and practise the dialogues.**

Lewis: Hi, Adam. Did you bring my computer game?

Adam: I'm sorry. I (**1**) left (**leave**) it at home this morning.

Lewis: Never mind. Did you have time to play it?

Adam: No, my dad (**2**) was using (**use**) the computer when I got home yesterday.

Lewis: It doesn't matter. Bring it tomorrow.

Judy: Hi, Adam. I want to say sorry. I forgot your birthday yesterday.

Adam: It's all right.

Judy: I (**3**) was going (**go**) to bed when I remembered! Did you have a party?

Adam: No, we (**4**) went (**go**) for a meal at a restaurant.

Judy: That's nice!

Speaking

4 Work in pairs. Look at the situations below and think of apologies. Then work with a new partner and make an apology. Use the *Useful expressions*. Take turns.

e.g. A: *I'm very sorry. I haven't got your magazine.*

1 you left a friend's magazine at home

2 you forgot a friend's birthday

3 you broke a friend's CD

4 you lost a friend's scarf

Writing: a biography

1 Judy wrote a biography of Amelia Earhart, her hero. Read the biography and find the following information about her.

1 date of birth / death
2 nationality ~~British~~ / American
3 appearance /
4 achievements /

2 Compete the biography with the words in the box.

> later   suddenly   then   when   when

3 Choose a famous person. Find out information and make notes using the ideas in Exercise 1. Then write a biography of the person.

Pronunciation: /ae/, /e/ and /ɜː/

5 4.7 Listen and repeat the words.

> bad   bed   bird   had   head   heard   and
> lend   learned   man   men   sand   send

6 4.8 Listen and choose the word you hear.

1 man — men
2 bad — bird
3 had — head
4 sand — send
5 ten — turn
6 land — learned

My hero - Amelia Earhart

Amelia Earhart was an American pilot. She was the first woman to fly across the Atlantic Ocean and the first person to fly from Hawaii to California.

Amelia was born in 1897. (1) *when* she was 23 years old, she flew in a small plane for the first time. (2) *suddenly*, she knew her ambition was to be a pilot. She learned to fly in 1921. (3) *then* she started to write magazine articles and books about flying. Amelia was very fashionable and elegant, but she cut her hair very short and she wore a leather jacket. She looked like a pilot.

In 1932, she flew across the Atlantic Ocean, and four years (4) *later* she decided to fly around the world. She disappeared in 1937 (5) *when* she was flying across the Pacific Ocean.

Culture Australia

Reading

1 **Work in pairs. Look at the photos and find these things.**

> an animal   a desert   a mountain
> a painting   a suit of armour

2 🔊4.9 **Read about Australian stories. Match the words in Exercise 1 with the paragraphs (1–3).**

3 **Read the text again and answer the questions.**

1 What is 'the dreamtime'?
2 What did Burke and Wills do?
3 Who was Ned Kelly?

Listening

4 🔊4.10 **Listen. Are the sentences true or false?**

1 Banjo Paterson was a writer and a poet.
2 He was born in 1864.
3 You can buy his book *The Man from Snowy River* today.
4 He recorded a song called *Waltzing Matilda*.

Australia is a country of stories. There are stories about the land and stories about the people.

1 Aboriginal people tell stories about the land and the beginning of the world – the dreamtime. In 'the dreamtime', animals, people and plants travelled across the land. Their activities and journeys created the land that we see today. The spirits of these ancient things still exist today. The aboriginal people tell these stories with songs, dances and special paintings.

2 Europeans arrived in Australia about 200 years ago. They have many stories about the heroic people from those times. One story is about two men called Burke and Wills. In 1860, they led an expedition to cross Australia from south to north. They didn't know that the centre of Australia is an enormous desert. They reached the north coast, but they died when they were returning to Melbourne.

3 The Australian criminal, Ned Kelly, was a hero to many writers, artists and ordinary people. His family had many problems with the police. Ned Kelly, with his brother and some friends, escaped. They lived in the 'bush' and many people helped them. Ned Kelly made armour to wear when he was fighting the police. But the police shot him in the leg and then they took him to prison. He was hanged in 1880.

Maths and English

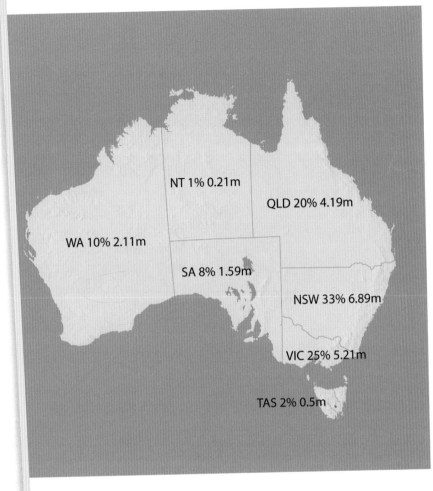

NT 1% 0.21m

QLD 20% 4.19m

WA 10% 2.11m

SA 8% 1.59m

NSW 33% 6.89m

VIC 25% 5.21m

TAS 2% 0.5m

1 **Look at the population map of Australia. How many states are there? Find the abbreviations for the names of the states.**

e.g. New South Wales N.S.W.
1 Northern Territory NT
2 Queensland QLD
3 South Australia SA
4 Tasmania TAS
5 Victoria VIC
6 Western Australia WA

2 **Are the sentences true or false?**

1 Twenty per cent of Australians live in Queensland. ✓ T
2 There are 500,000 people in Tasmania. ✗ 6840l. F
3 More than fifty per cent of the population live in Western Australia. ✗ F
4 The population of Western Australia is ten times the population of the Northern Territory. ✓ T
5 Twenty-five per cent of Australians live in Victoria. ✓ T.

Project

Choose a story that is important in your country. It can be about a person, a place, or a traditional story. Write a paragraph. Say what the story is about, when you heard it for the first time and why you like it.

Review Units 3 and 4

Vocabulary

1 Write words connected with mass media.

1 read a n.............
2 listen to a r............ programme
3 watch a t............ programme
4 write an e.............
5 read a m.............

1 mark per item: …/5 marks

2 What type of film … ?

1 tells a love story — *Love articles.*
2 has animated drawings — *Cartoon*
3 is funny — *Comedy film*
4 is frightening — *Horror film*
5 is about the future — *Technology film*

1 mark per item: …/5 marks

3 Write the verbs about life events.

1 g..el..up
2 l..eave..school
3 p..ess..an exam
4 g..et..a job
5 h..ave..a family

1 mark per item: …/5 marks

4 Choose the correct words in the description.

The man has got
(**1**) blue / green eyes. His
hair is (**2**) long / short,
(**3**) dark / fair and
(**4**) curly / straight. He's also
got a (**5**) beard / moustache.

1 mark per item: …/5 marks

5 Write the adjectives.

1 That film was very *confusing* . (**confuse**)
2 I'm *boring* Let's go for a walk. (**bore**)
3 The exam was hard! I'm *tiring* (**tire**)
4 I think horror stories are *frightening* (**frighten**)
5 Didn't you win the competition? I'm .... !
(**surprise**) — *surprising.*

1 mark per item: …/5 marks

Grammar

6 Complete the sentences with the past simple form of be.

1 They *was* at the cinema last night. (✔)
2 He *was* at school yesterday. (✗)
3 You *were* at the concert on Saturday. (✗)
4 I '*m* fifteen last week. (✔)
5 She *was* funny in that film. (✔)

1 mark per item: …/5 marks

7 Write past simple questions.

1 .... her a card? (**you / send**)
2 .... at her party? (**they / be**)
3 .... hieroglyphics? (**the Egyptians / use**)
4 .... an inventor? (**Gutenberg / be**)
5 .... the information on the Internet? (**she / find**)

1 mark per item: …/5 marks

8 Complete the sentences with the past simple form of the verbs.

1 Yesterday I *get up* at six o'clock in the morning.
(**wake up**)
2 My friend *buy* a jacket yesterday. (**buy**)
3 The robber *steal* a car. (**steal**)
4 Romeo and Juliet *fell* in love. (**fall**)
5 The writer *win* prize for his first book. (**win**)

1 mark per item: …/5 marks

9 Complete the paragraph with the past simple or past continuous form of the verbs.

While we (**1**) *walking* (**walk**) to school yesterday,
we (**2**) *find* (**find**) a dog. It (**3**) *having* (**have**) beautiful
brown eyes. It (**4**) *bing* (**be**) lost, so we
(**5**) *taking* (**take**) it to the police station.

1 mark per item: …/5 marks

10 Complete the sentences.

1 '*what* did Shrek marry?'
'Princess Fiona.'
2 '............ did the Hobbits go with Frodo?'
'To protect him.'
3 They made that film ....*in*.. 2008.
4 I read the book two years ...*old*..
5 We were cycling .... the rain started.

1 mark per item: …/5 marks

Communicate

11 Complete the dialogue with these expressions.

> I agree   I don't agree   Me too   No way
> What do you think

Jill: What did you do at the weekend, Damian?
Damian: We saw *Rambo*. It was great.
Jill: (1) *I agree*! I think it's boring and violent.
Damian: Really? (2) *I don't agree* Neil?
Neil: (3) *Me too* with Jill. I don't like violent films.
Jill: I prefer musicals.
Neil: (4) *What do you think*.
Damian: Well, (5) *No way* sorry.

2 marks per item: .../10 marks

12 Match the statements with the responses.

1 I enjoyed the concert.
2 I'm sorry. I forgot your book.
3 What's your opinion, Jill?
4 Hey, that's my book, not yours.
5 I'm sorry I'm late.

a I agree with you. It's boring.
b It's all right. What happened?
c Me too!
d Never mind. Bring it tomorrow.
e Oh! I'm sorry.

2 marks per item: .../10 marks

13 Choose the correct sound for each verb ending.

1 appeared   /t/   /d/   /ɪd/
2 chased   /t/   /d/   /ɪd/
3 enjoyed   /t/   /d/   /ɪd/
4 listened   /t/   /d/   /ɪd/
5 looked   /t/   /d/   /ɪd/
6 painted   /t/   /d/   /ɪd/
7 received   /t/   /d/   /ɪd/
8 showed   /t/   /d/   /ɪd/
9 used   /t/   /d/   /ɪd/
10 walked   /t/   /d/   /ɪd/

1 mark per item: .../10 marks

14 Choose the two words in each group with a different vowel sound.

e.g. land   left   when   *land*

1 bad   bed   head
2 bird   had   heard
3 sand   said   send
4 learn ten   turn
5 man   men   that

2 marks per item: .../10 marks

15 Complete the story with the words in the box.

> had his later my to was when
> while wrote years

My uncle isn't famous, but he's (1) .... hero. Two (2) .... ago, he went on holiday (3) .... Scotland. While he was there, he (4) .... an accident. He was climbing in ice and snow, (5) .... he fell. He broke (6) .... back. (7) .... he was waiting for help, a snowstorm began. Seven hours (8) .... , a doctor arrived. My uncle (9) .... in hospital for six months. He (10) .... a really funny blog every day. I think he's amazing.

1 mark per item: .../10 marks

Total: .../100

I can...

I can express and ask for opinions.
I can agree and disagree.
I can make and accept apologies.
I can tell stories.

Film review

Reading

1 Read the film review and answer the question.

TRANSFORMERS
REVENGE OF THE FALLEN

1 *Transformers: Revenge of the Fallen* is a science fiction action film. It came out in 2009. The director was Michael Bay.

2 The story is about a war between the Autobots and the Decepticons. They are robots but Sam, the hero, is human. The Fallen is the leader of the Decepticons and he wants to kill everyone on Earth. The action takes place in different countries like Jordan, Egypt, France and the USA.

3 I thought the film was exciting and the special effects were amazing. But I think there were two problems with the film. Firstly, the story was very long and confusing. I didn't always understand what was happening while I was watching it. Secondly, I thought the film was frightening. It's not a good film for young children.

1 What is the title of the film?
2 What kind of film is it?
3 Who directed it?

4 Who is in the film?
5 What is the story about?
6 Where does the action happen?

7 What did the writer like about the film?
8 What are the two problems with the film?

In which paragraphs does the writer include the things below?

The things that happen in the film
Where the action happens
The name of the film
Who is in the film
The name of the director
What the writer thinks of the film

Project

Write a review of a film you liked.

- Write the name of the film and any important information
- Say what kind of film it is (cartoon / fantasy / musical, etc)
- Try to find out the names of the characters or the director
- Write about the plot (say what happens in the story)
- Write about the good and bad things about the film
- Say if you think people will like it
- Try to find some pictures of the film from magazines or the Internet and make your review look exciting

NATIONAL GEOGRAPHIC

World records

5

> **Grammar**

Learn about comparative and superlative adjectives, *too* and *enough,* and *have to.*

> **Vocabulary**

Learn words for animals, and habitats.

> **Skills**

Read about giraffes, extreme places, and the Okavango Delta.

Listen to an interview about caves.

Write a quiz.

> **Communicate**

Buy things in shops.

1 Work in pairs. Look at the photo of a Bristlecone pine tree. How old do you think it is?

   a 40 years old **b** 400 years old **c** 4,000 years old

2 ○5.1 **Listen to the conversation about a TV programme and answer the questions.**

   1 What was the programme about?

   2 What was special about the trees and the tortoises?

3 Work in pairs. How many pets can you name?

4 Have you got a pet? Tell your partner about your pet – or about a pet you'd like to have.

See Vocabulary Explorer: Page 106

55

Giraffes – the giants of the savannah

Giraffes are incredibly tall. In fact, giraffes are taller than all the other animals in the world. Adult giraffes can grow to six metres – that's taller than a typical house! Baby giraffes are about two metres tall when they are born – they're bigger than an adult human. This incredible height gives giraffes an important advantage on the savannah because they can see when lions are in the area. That's why you can often see antelopes and zebras with giraffes. It's less dangerous than being alone.

Giraffes are 'giant-sized' in many ways. Adult giraffes weigh 850–1,270 kilograms. That's heavier than a family car! And they have an enormous appetite – adults eat about 60 kilograms of leaves every day. They take leaves off tall trees with their 53-centimetre-long tongues. Their large feet are wider than dinner plates.

Perhaps surprisingly, giraffes are very fast. Even baby giraffes can run at about 50 kilometres per hour. That's quicker than Lance Armstrong's average speed in the Tour de France, but it's slower than a cheetah. Cheetahs can run at 80 kilometres per hour. Luckily for giraffes, cheetahs aren't strong enough to attack them – the giraffes are too heavy. In fact, only lions are strong enough to attack young or weak giraffes. Thanks to its giant size, a giraffe's life is better than many other savannah animals.

Vocabulary

1 5.2 **Work in pairs. Ask and answer the questions. Then listen and check your answers.**

   1 How heavy are killer whales?
      a   5,400 kg   b   2,600 kg
   2 How long is a green anaconda?
      a   5.5 m   b   8.8 m
   3 How big are ants?
      a   2–25 mm   b   15–40 mm
   4 How wide are African elephants' ears?
      a   1 m   b   2 m
   5 How tall are giraffes?
      a   3 m   b   6 m

   See Vocabulary Explorer: Page 106

Reading and listening

2 5.3 **Read and listen to the text. Answer the questions.**

   1 Where do giraffes live?
   2 What do giraffes eat?
   3 Which animals attack giraffes?

3 **Read the text again and complete the sentences.**

   1 Giraffes can weigh …
   2 Their tongues are …
   3 Baby giraffes can run at …

Grammar: comparative adjectives

4 Complete the table with the words in the box.

better   happier   less   longer

	Adjective	Comparative
One syllable	long hot large	(1) .... hotter larger
Ending in y	happy lucky	(2) .... luckier
Two or more syllables	important	more / (3) .... important
Irregular	good bad	(4) .... worse

See Grammar Explorer: Page 125

5 Find the comparative forms of these adjectives in the text.

big   dangerous   heavy
quick   slow   tall   wide

6 Complete the sentences with comparative forms of the adjectives.

e.g. Cheetahs are *faster* than lions. (fast)

1 Lions are .... than humans. (**strong**)
2 The savannah is .... than a zoo. (**dangerous**)
3 Animals are .... than plants. (**active**)
4 My English is .... than my French. (**good**)
5 I'm .... than you at sport. (**bad**)

7 Write true sentences about the pairs of animals.

e.g. lions / cheetahs (slow) *Lions are slower than cheetahs.*

1 elephants / zebras (**big**)
2 crocodiles / giraffes (**dangerous**)
3 cows / gorillas (**intelligent**)
4 cats / bears (**small**)
5 whales / sharks (**heavy**)

8 Write questions about the animals in the Vocabulary Explorer on page 106. Use the adjectives in the box in the comparative form. Then work with a partner. Ask and answer the questions.

e.g. A: *Which is bigger – a hamster or a mouse?*
B: *I think a hamster is bigger than a mouse.*

big   dangerous   friendly   intelligent
long   poisonous   small   ugly

9 Work in pairs.

A: Think of a number between 1 and 100. Don't tell your partner.
B: Try to guess the number. Take turns. Then continue using the ideas below.

e.g. B: *34?*   **A:** *bigger*
B: *67?*   **A:** *smaller*

a temperature (0–100 °C): hotter / colder

a person in your class: taller / shorter

a person you both know: older / younger

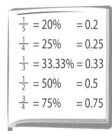

$\frac{1}{5} = 20\% = 0.2$
$\frac{1}{4} = 25\% = 0.25$
$\frac{1}{3} = 33.33\% = 0.33$
$\frac{1}{2} = 50\% = 0.5$
$\frac{3}{4} = 75\% = 0.75$

a school subject: easier / more difficult

Working with words

10 Look at the examples. Then write true sentences with the adjectives in brackets.

Cheetahs aren't strong enough to attack giraffes.
Cheetahs are too weak to attack giraffes.

1 The baby giraffe didn't eat the leaves. It (short).
2 I didn't touch the snake. I (brave).
3 I can't do physics. It (difficult).
4 He didn't win the race. He (fast).

See Grammar Explorer: Page 125

🕐 *Fast finishers*

Look at the animals in the Vocabulary Explorer on page 106 for two minutes. Close your book. How many animals can you write down in one minute? Repeat. Can you do better?

From English 2 Explorer Cengage Helen Stephenson 2016.

EXTREME EXPLORER TRIPS OF A LIFETIME!

Jump from the highest waterfall.

Explore the deepest cave.
Trek across the hottest desert.

Sleep on the coldest continent.
Dive in the largest reef.

Sail the biggest river.

Vocabulary

1 Work in pairs. Tick (✓) the places that you have in your country. Can you name some of them?

- a cave   a desert
- a forest   a lake
- a mountain   a river
- a valley   a waterfall

See Vocabulary Explorer: Page 107

Reading and listening

2 ○ 5.4 Read and listen to the text. Which places in Exercise 1 are in the text?

Are you looking for an extreme experience? Are you tough enough for the most difficult conditions on Earth?

What's your wildest dream? Base jumping 979 metres from Angel Falls or going 2.1 kilometres underground into Krubera Cave?
Get ready for the most exciting experience of your life!

Perhaps you prefer a drier place, like a desert – how about trekking across the Sahara in 58°C? Or how about Antarctica? It's the most hostile desert with only 5 cm rain a year and temperatures of –80°C. It isn't warm enough for plants or animals to survive. Is this the worst place on Earth for a holiday?

Alternatively, dive in the Great Barrier Reef in Australia. Tiny animals – corals – make coral reefs, and this is the largest coral reef in the world. Or sail down the Amazon River – 20 per cent of all the Earth's fresh water is in this river. Follow the river across South America, through the world's largest rainforest, and have the best holiday possible.

3

the highest
the deepest
the biggest

h

Grammar: superlative adjectives

4 Complete the table with superlative adjectives from the text.

	Adjective	Superlative
One syllable	high hot	the (**1**) *highest* the (**2**) *hottest*
Ending in *y*	dry	the driest
Two or more syllables	difficult	the (**3**) *most difficult* / least difficult
Irregular	good bad	the best the (**4**) ....

(handwritten: most difficult / difficultest x)

See Grammar Explorer: Page 125

5 How many superlative adjectives can you find in the text? Work in pairs and compare with your partner.

6 Write sentences about the places in the text. Use superlative adjectives.

e.g. *Angel Falls is the highest waterfall in the world.*

7 Write the superlative forms of the adjectives. Then complete the sentences with your ideas.

e.g. *Coldplay* are the *best* band in the world. (**good**)

1 .... is the .... singer in the world. (**bad**)
2 .... is the .... sport. (**dangerous**)
3 .... is the .... subject at school. (**easy**)
4 .... is the .... place for a holiday. (**interesting**)
5 .... was the .... film last year. (**exciting**)

8 Work in pairs. Compare your sentences from Exercise 7.

e.g. **A:** *Coldplay are the best band in the world.*
  B: *Really? I think Franz Ferdinand are better! They're the best band in the world.*

Listening

9 5.5 Listen to an interview with a photographer. Which of the places on the webpage is he talking about?

10 5.5 Listen to the interview again and find out about the special preparations that are necessary. Are the sentences true or false?

1 Cavers have to wear special clothes. ✗ *true*
2 Cavers don't have to wear helmets. ✓ *false*
3 Cavers have to wear lights on their heads. ✗ *true*
4 In Krubera Cave, people have to sleep ✗ underground.
5 You have to do special training to camp in a cave. ✓

Grammar: *have to*

11 Choose the correct option to make true sentences.

1 Cavers **have to** / don't have to take lights into caves. = It's necessary.
2 Cavers have to / **don't have to** do special training. = It's not necessary.
3 Do cavers in Krubera have to camp underground? **Yes, they do** / No, they don't. = It's necessary.

See Grammar Explorer: Page 125–126

12 Work in pairs. Decide if the things are necessary or unnecessary. Then write sentences with *have to / don't have to*.

e.g. cavers / wear helmets *Cavers have to wear helmets.*

1 base-jumpers / wear a parachute *Cavers have to wear a parachute.*
2 divers / use lights *Cavers don't have to use lights*
3 mountain climbers / sleep on the mountain
4 teachers / do special training *Cavers have to mountain climbers Cavers have to do special training.*
5 we / wear a school uniform *Wear have to school uniform.*

Study skills

Use different methods to help you remember new words.

Look at the examples for *helmet*.

1 Write a sentence: *You wear a helmet in a cave or on a motorbike.*

2 Draw a picture of it.

3 Write it with a group of similar words. *helmet, jacket, boots, gloves*

Reading and listening

1 **Look at the photo. Where are Adam, Lewis, Judy and Kate?**

   a in a bookshop

   b in a supermarket

   c in a sports shop

2 5.6 **Read and listen to the dialogue. Does Adam buy the boots?**

Assistant:	Can I help you?
Adam:	Yes, I'm looking for some boots.
Assistant:	OK, boots are over here.
Lewis:	Look, these are good!
Adam:	Yeah! How much are they?
Assistant:	They're £65.
Adam:	Wow! They're a bit too expensive.
Assistant:	Well, this pair is cheaper.
Lewis:	And I think they're better than the first pair – I like the colour.
Adam:	Can I try them on?
Assistant:	Yes, of course. What size are you?
Adam:	I'm a size eight.
Assistant:	Here you are.
Adam:	Thanks.
Lewis:	How are they? Are they big enough?
Adam:	They're too big. Have you got a smaller size?
Assistant:	Not at the moment, I'm afraid – perhaps on Saturday.
Adam:	That's all right. I can come back then.

3 Look at the *Useful expressions*. Write C for customer or A for assistant next to each expression.

USEFUL EXPRESSIONS

Can I help you?
Yes, I'm looking for some boots.
How much is it / are they?
It's / They're £65.
What size are you?
I'm a size eight.
Can I try it / them on?
Yes, of course.
Is it / Are they big enough?
It's / They're too big.

4 Kate wants to buy some things in the shop. Complete the dialogue. Use the dialogue in Exercise 2, the words in brackets and the *Useful expressions* to help you.

Assistant: (**1**) ....?
Kate: Yes, I'm looking for some trousers.
Assistant: (**2**) ....
Kate: Oh, thanks. How much are they?
Assistant: (**3**) ....
Kate: OK. Can I try them on?
Assistant: (**4**) ....
Kate: They're a bit big.
Assistant: (**5**) .... (smaller)
Kate: Yes, these are great.
Assistant: Good.

Listening

5 5.7 Listen to three conversations. Match the conversations (1–3) with three of the places (a–e).

Pronunciation: intonation in questions with question words

6 5.8 Listen and repeat the questions.

1   How long is the film?
2   How much are the sandwiches?
3   What size are you?
4   When does it finish?
5   Where are the dictionaries?
6   Who's in this film?

Speaking

7 Work in pairs. You are in the places in Exercise 5. Take turns to be the customer and the assistant. Buy these things or use your own ideas. Use some of the questions from Exercise 6.

> a dictionary   a hamster   a milkshake
> a rabbit   a sandwich   a pair of trainers
> a T-shirt   tickets for *Madagascar 2*

Writing: a quiz

1 Put the words in order to make questions.

1   highest / is / the / the / mountain / Which / in / world?
2   in / country / is / Which / it?
3   high / How / it / is?
4   was / to / the / the / When / first / successful / expedition / top?

2 Choose the correct answer to each question in Exercise 1.

1   Mount Kilimanjaro / Mount Everest / K2
2   Afghanistan / Nepal / India
3   6,654m / 8,543m / 11,877m
4   1923 / 1953 / 1983

3 Write ten questions for a quiz. Write three options for each answer. Choose from the ideas below and use your own ideas. Find the information in reference books and on the Internet. Do your quiz with a partner.

> the biggest city
> the fastest vehicle
> the most dangerous animal
> the most expensive place
> the oldest animal
> the richest person
> the smallest country
> the tallest building

Reading

1 Work in pairs. Look at the photos and find these things.

baskets elephants hippopotamuses
people a plane a river sand trees

2 ⊙5.9 Read about the Okavango Delta. Match the descriptions (1–4) with the photos (a–d).

Listening

3 ⊙5.10 Listen and match the descriptions with the animals.

Culture

Botswana

1 A plane takes tourists on an eco-safari over the Okavango Delta in Botswana. The Okavango River begins 1,600 kilometres to the north. Most rivers go to the sea, but the Okavango ends in the Kalahari Desert! The delta covers 17,000 square kilometres and it's the largest inland delta in the world. It's called a delta because the river ends in many smaller rivers and lakes.

2 People and animals depend on the water of the Okavango. Both men and women go fishing in the delta. Men go out on boats and use nets. Women make baskets from palm leaves and they put the baskets underwater. Then the children chase the fish into the baskets.

3 The delta attracts many different animals. Some need water to drink and others live in water. Hippopotamuses, for example, spend a lot of time resting in water. The water also helps plants to grow and many animals eat these plants. The delta can be a dangerous place for plant-eating animals. Lions, leopards and cheetahs are never far away.

4 Elephants are the largest land animals. Only giraffes are taller than elephants. Botswana has the biggest elephant population on Earth. The elephants are important to the people and other animals in the delta. In the dry season, the river can almost disappear. The elephants dig in the sand and find water in underground streams.

a

b

c

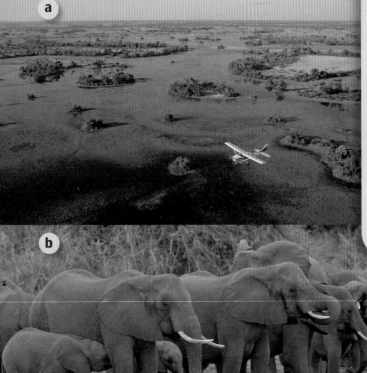

d

Geography and English
The continents

1 Look at the map. Can you find these places? Look carefully!

| Africa | Asia | Australia | North America | South America |

2 Read about the movement of the continents. Are the sentences true or false?

1 Laurasia broke up into Pangaea and Gondwana. ~~Gondwana was to the south.~~ ~~True~~ *false*

2 Part of Gondwana moved north and crashed into Laurasia. *False True*

3 After the continents separated, plants and animals developed in different ways. ~~False~~ ~~False~~ *True*

Millions of years ago, the land on Earth was one giant continent. Scientists call this Pangaea. Then about 170 million years ago, Pangaea broke up. This made two new continents – Laurasia and Gondwana.

Laurasia was in the area of the equator and Gondwana was to the south. About 150 million years ago, parts of Gondwana separated. To the west, South America broke off from Africa. To the east, a large area of land moved north. Eventually this crashed into Laurasia and the violence of this made the Himalaya mountains.

Gondwana and Laurasia separated and moved apart into new continents. That's why we can find similar animals and plants on different continents. But the continents continued to move. Plants and animals on one continent developed in one way and plants and animals on a different continent developed in another way. In many places, especially islands, there are animals and plants that only exist in one place. However, the continents are still moving a few centimetres each year. The process continues.

Project

Find out about a special animal in your country. Make a poster to show the animal, its habitat, and other information about it.

Exploring the Amazon

1 What do you know about the Amazon? Discuss the questions with a partner before you read the article.

1 Where is it?
2 What is the land like?
3 What kind of people lived there 100 years ago?
4 What problems do the native people have with the modern world?

2 Read the text and match the words (1-10) to their meanings (a-j).

1	tribes	a	adventurous journey
2	expedition	b	groups of people
3	wildest	c	something that shows people think you're important
4	rainforest	d	leader
5	honour	e	opposite of war
6	national park	f	area with many trees
7	peace	g	party or celebration
8	separate	h	opposite of together
9	chief	i	most difficult to travel through
10	festival	j	protected area for animals or people

3 Answer these questions with a word or a short phrase.

1 When was the Roncador-Xingu expedition?
2 What was the expedition doing?
3 What did they do when they met Indians?
4 When did the park open?
5 How many Indians were living in the park in the 1990s?
6 When did the brothers die?
7 What was Claudio doing when he died?
8 What happened when Orlando died?

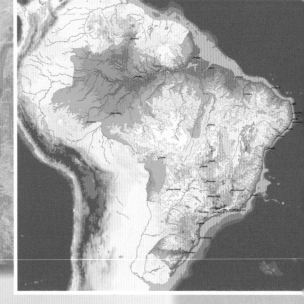

The Villas-Boas brothers

Claudio Villas-Boas and his two brothers, Orlando and Leonardo, spent most of their lives trying to help the native Indian tribes in Brazil. In 1943, the brothers joined the Roncador-Xingu expedition which was exploring the land deep in Amazonia.

Amazonia is one of the wildest areas in the world – it was too dangerous for most people to go there in those days. The Villas-Boas brothers had many problems while they were travelling, and they had to be clever to make friends with the Indians they met.

In 1961 the Xingu National Park opened. This was a place where Indians could live in peace, separate from the other Brazilians and far away from the modern world. 30 years later, 6,000 Indians were living there and it was one of the biggest parks of its kind. Leonardo was younger than the other two brothers, but he died in 1961 and did not live long enough to see this.

Claudio wrote 13 books with Orlando and he was writing another book when he died in 1998. One tribal chief said of Claudio, 'Now our father is gone'. When Orlando died in 2002, the Xingu Indians held a great festival called the Kuarup. This is one of the biggest honours – especially for a white man.

Some of the tribes the brothers contacted:

Kalapalos
Kayabi
Kamaiuros
Meinacos
Txucarramoes
Kreen-Akarore or Panaros

The brothers were nominated for the Nobel Peace Prize in 1973.

Sports and games

> Grammar

Learn about *must/mustn't,* and countable and uncountable nouns.

> Vocabulary

Learn words for sports and games, and food.

> Skills

Read about a race, food on expeditions, and extreme sports.

Listen to a food expert talking about diet.

Write about your favourite sport.

> Communicate

Ask for and give permission.

1 Work in pairs. How do you think the man feels?

2 Discuss the photo. What do you think about this sport? Choose words from the box.

> amazing   boring   exciting
> frightening   interesting

3 6.1 Listen to the conversation. What sports and games do the boys do at their schools?

See Vocabulary Explorer: Page 108

4 Work in pairs. Tell your partner about the sports and games you:

like playing   like watching   play at home
play at school   watch on television

The 4 Deserts race

The **4 Deserts** race is the most difficult race on Earth. The race has four parts. Each part is in a different desert – the Atacama in Chile, the Gobi in China, the Sahara in Africa and, finally, Antarctica. Competitors must run or walk 250 kilometres through each desert. Competitors must finish the first three parts successfully. Then they can compete in the fourth and final part.

Competition rules

1   You must be 21 years old or over.
2   You must finish the race in seven days.
3   You must follow the official route of the race.
4   You must carry your own food and clothes.
5   You must not drop any litter on the route.
6   You must not touch any plants or rocks on the route.
7   You must sleep at the official campsites.
8   You must wear a small nationality flag on your arm.
9   You must not wear adverts on your clothes.
10 You must not use video cameras or mobile phones.

Reading and listening

1   6.2 **Read and listen to the information about the *4 Deserts* race and choose the correct answers.**

1   How many parts are there in the race?

a   two

b   three

c   four

2   Where is the race?

a   in Chile and China

b   in Africa and Antarctica

c   in all four places

3   How do the competitors race?

a   by bicycle

b   on foot

c   by motorbike

2   **Read the competition rules again. Why can't these people take part in the race? Write the competitors' names and the rule numbers.**

e.g. Simon – 6.

Simon   Emma   Daniel

Grammar: *must* and *mustn't*

3   **Look at the examples. Then rewrite the sentences.**

e.g. Don't drop litter. You must not (mustn't) drop litter.

Wear your flag on your arm. You must wear your flag on your arm.

1   Carry your own food. cereal

2   Don't use video cameras. phones

3   Don't touch plants or rocks. touch adverts

4   Don't wear adverts on your clothes.

5   Follow the official route.
drop

Must and *mustn't* is the same for *I, you, he, she, it, we* and *they.*

See Grammar Explorer: Page 126

4 Match the sentences (1–6) with the signs (a–d).

1 Walkers and runners must use the walkway. _c_
2 You mustn't feed the animals. _b_
3 You mustn't leave your pet in your car. _d_
4 Cyclists and skaters must use the bikeway. _C_
5 You mustn't take photos. _a_
6 You mustn't go near the animals. _b_

Grammar: *can/can't* and *must/mustn't*

5 Read the questions (1–6) about the *4 Deserts* race. Match the questions with the correct answers (a–f).

1 I'm 21 next year. Can I take part in the race now? _c_
2 Can I decide the best route to take across the desert? _e_
3 Can I wear my country flag on my back? _d_
4 Can I take photos with my mobile phone? _b_
5 Can I sleep in my own tent? _f_
6 Can I take a week to complete the race? _a_

a No, you can't. Competitors mustn't leave the official route. See rule 3. _6_
b No. You mustn't use mobile phones for phone calls or for photography. See rule 10. _4_
~~c~~ No. You must be 21 or over to take part in the race. See rule 1.
d No. You must wear your flag on your arm. See rule 8. _3_
e Yes, you can take seven days. See rule 2. _2_
f No, you can't. Competitors must sleep at the official campsites. See rule 7. _5_

See Grammar Explorer: Page 126

Vocabulary

6 Work in pairs. Match the sports and games in the box with the sentences. Then complete the sentences with *must, mustn't* or *can*.

> cards   ~~chess~~   ~~football~~   table tennis   tennis

1 You _chess_ move each piece the correct way.
2 You .... touch the ball with your hands.
3 You .... look at the other player's cards.
4 You _football_ play with two or four players.
5 You .... put your hand on the table.

See Vocabulary Explorer: Page 108

7 Work in pairs. Choose a sport or game from Vocabulary Explorer, page 108. How many sentences can you make? Try to use *must, mustn't* and *can*.

Working with words

8 Look at the examples from the text. Make nouns from the verbs in the table.

Can we compete as a team?

Competitors must be 21 years old or over.

Read the competition rules.

	-ation, -tion	-er, -or
explore, inform, invent, investigate	*exploration*	*explorer*
celebrate, imagine, predict, prepare	preparation	

9 Complete the sentences with words from Exercise 8.

1 The carnival in Rio de Janeiro is a spectacular ....
2 Who was the .... of the printing press?
3 When you do extreme sports, careful .... is very important.
4 We can find .... quickly on the Internet.
5 She writes great stories. She has a fantastic ....

Fast finishers

Find the odd word out in each list. Then write more lists for a partner.

1 basketball   football   handball   volleyball
2 badminton   darts   squash   tennis
3 bowling   cards   chess   draughts
4 dominoes   football   hockey   rugby

Expedition food

In May 1953, Edmund Hillary and Tenzing Norgay were the first climbers to reach the top of Everest. The conditions were incredibly difficult. It's extremely cold and very difficult to breathe at high altitudes. Hillary and Tenzing took a lot of oxygen, in bottles, to help them breathe. But they didn't have any modern technology like GPS or mobile phones. Their clothes were heavy and old-fashioned, but they were warm. And there was no fresh food. They only had tins and packets of powdered food.

The night before they climbed the final section, they camped at 8,500 metres. They drank a lot of tea with a lot of sugar in it. They ate some tins of fish and some biscuits. The next day, they reached the top of the mountain. Hillary took off his oxygen mask. There was some ice on his camera, but he took some photos. Fifteen minutes later, they started to go down again. When they reached their tent, Hillary sat down and ate two omelettes and some fish. He drank a litre of lemonade too.

Reading and listening

1 Work in pairs. Imagine you are on the expedition in the photo. Which things are most important? Why?

> a camera   food   a GPS   a mobile phone
> oxygen   a tent   warm clothes

2 ⊙ 6.3 Read and listen to the text about the first successful expedition to the top of Everest. Which things from Exercise 1 did the climbers take?

Vocabulary

3 Read the text again and find six things that Hillary and Norgay ate and drank.

4 Match the food items in the box with their containers (1–6). You can match some food items with more than one container.

beans	biscuits	cereal	coffee	eggs	jam
juice	lemonade	milk	oil	rice	sugar

1 bottles of   3 cans of   5 jars of

2 boxes of   4 cartons of   6 packets of

See Vocabulary Explorer: Page 109

Grammar: countable and uncountable nouns

5 Complete the table with the words from Exercise 4.

Countable nouns: bottles, ... Uncountable nouns: oil, ...

> Countable nouns can be singular (*a box*) or plural (*boxes*). Uncountable nouns have only one form.

See Grammar Explorer: Page 126

6 Write *a* or *an* where necessary.

e.g. He drank *a* cup of tea.

1 Do you want .... biscuit with your tea?

2 I love .... cheese.

3 He made .... omelette.

Grammar: *some, any* and *no*

7 Complete the table with *some, any* or *no*.

Affirmative		
They ate There was There were	(1)	biscuits. ice. tins of fish.
Negative		
They didn't have There wasn't There weren't	(2)	modern technology. fresh food. mobile phones.
Negative		
They had There was There were	(3)	warm clothes. fresh food. apples.
Questions		
Did they take Was there Were there	any	cheese? fresh food? mobile phones?

> **The past tense of** *there is/are* **is** *there was/were*.

See Grammar Explorer: Page 126

8 Complete the text with *some, any* or *no*.

Last week our geography class went on a trip. It was a very hot day. There were (**1**) *no* clouds in the sky. I didn't have (**2**) .... sun cream, so I got sunburnt. We walked for an hour and we looked at (**3**) .... rock formations. The teacher took (**4**) .... photos, and then we had a picnic. I was thirsty because I had (**5**) .... water with me. There weren't (**6**) .... cafes. My friend gave me (**7**) .... juice and (**8**) .... fruit.

Listening

9 ⊙ 6.4 **Choose the correct answers. Then listen to a food expert and check your answers.**

1 How much fruit is best in a normal diet?
a lot / not much

2 How much meat is best in a normal diet?
a lot / not much

3 How much energy do people on expeditions use?
a lot / not much

4 How many calories does pasta have?
a lot / not many

5 How much energy do we get from eating pasta?
a lot / not much

10 ⊙ 6.4 **Listen again and complete the sentences with *a lot of* and *not much*.**

1 People on expeditions can eat .... food like biscuits and chocolate because they use .... energy.

2 In ordinary life, the best diet includes .... fruit and vegetables but .... sugar.

Study skills

Learning new grammatical forms

1 **Write your own sentences with new grammatical forms. It helps you to remember them. Look at the examples.**

e.g. They ate <u>some fish</u>.

> I ate <u>some yoghurt</u> this morning.

There were <u>no apples</u>.

> There were <u>no lions</u> at the zoo.

2 **Look at the Grammar Explorer on page 126 and this page again. Write your own sentences in your notebook. Use *must/mustn't, can/can't*, and *some, any, no*.**

6C Permission

Reading and listening

X1 6.5 **Read and listen to the dialogue. Judy and Kate ask permission to do three things. What do they say?**

Teacher: That's all for today. Don't forget to bring your finished projects on Wednesday.

Judy: Can I ask a question, sir?

Teacher: Yes, of course, Judy.

Judy: Do we have to hand in our projects on Wednesday?

Teacher: Yes, you do. That's the deadline.

Judy: Oh.

Kate: But sir, can we hand them in on Friday?

Teacher: No, I'm afraid you can't. All Year 8 projects must be on my desk on Wednesday.

Kate: Do I have to print my project? Can't I email it to you?

Teacher: Is there a problem?

Kate: Well, sir, it's really difficult to print out our projects. There was no paper in the school printer this morning.

Judy: We have to ask the librarian for paper, but she's not here this week.

Teacher: Hmm, that's a bit of a problem. OK, you can email your projects on Wednesday, but you must give me the printed copies on Friday.

Judy: Thank you, sir!

Teacher: You're welcome.

LIBRARY RULES

NO food, drink or conversation

Ask the librarian for:
- Computer access codes
- Paper for the printer
- Photocopier key

2 Look at the school library rules. Choose the correct answers to the student's questions.

1 Can I use my own paper in the printer?
   a Yes, of course.
   b No, you can't. You must use the school's paper.

2 Can I go on the Internet?
   a Yes, of course. Here's your computer access code.
   b No, you can't.

3 📀 **6.6 Listen and repeat the *Useful expressions*. Focus on your intonation.**

USEFUL EXPRESSIONS

Can I ask a question?
Can't I email it … ?
Do we have to … ?
Yes, of course.
No, I'm afraid you can't.
Yes, you do.
No, you don't.
You can …, but you must …

Speaking

4 **Look at the ideas (a–g). You want permission to do these things. Who do you ask? Write T for teacher or P for parents next to each thing.**

a go back to the classroom
b stay at your best friend's house tonight
c have some extra time for homework
d invite some friends to lunch
e eat cough sweets in class
f lend your Playstation to a friend
g go home early

Writing: a sports event

1 **Lewis wrote about his favourite sport for the school magazine. Read the paragraph and answer the questions.**

1 What's the sport?
2 When does he do it?
3 Who does he do it with?
4 What's the most famous event in the sport?
5 Who is a famous person in the sport?
6 Why is it his favourite sport/event?
7 What happened at the last event?

2 **Look at the examples from the paragraph. Then match the sentence beginnings (1–3) with the logical endings (a–c).**

e.g. I really love cycling, so I go every day.

Last year the route was easier, so there weren't any serious accidents.

1 My brother is in a swimming team,
2 It rained all weekend,
3 Tennis is my favourite sport,

a so I always watch Wimbledon.
b so we didn't go out.
c so he trains every day.

3 **Write a paragraph about your favourite sport. Use the questions from Exercise 1 to help you plan your paragraph.**

5 **Work in pairs. Practise asking for and giving or refusing permission. Use the ideas in Exercise 4 and the *Useful expressions*. Take turns.**

e.g. A: *Sir, can I go home early today?*
B: *Why?*
A: *Well, I have to go to the dentist's.*
B: *No, you can't. / Yes, you can … , but you must …*

Pronunciation: /s/ and /z/

6 📀 **6.7 Listen to each pair of words. Do they sound the same (S) or different (D)?**

1 ice — eyes
2 race — rays
3 rice — rise

7 📀 **6.8 Say each word. Then listen, check and repeat.**

cheese	chess	days	jars	glass	photos
plays	price	prize	use	years	was

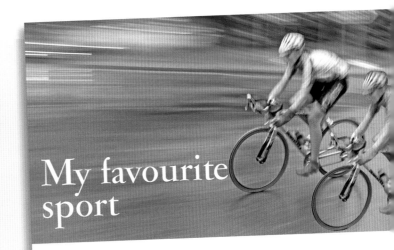

My favourite sport

I really love cycling, so I go out every day and sometimes twice a day! My sister often comes with me. I think the best race is the Tour de France. The race is in France, but the competitors are from a lot of different countries. There are some excellent cyclists this year, but my favourite (and my hero) is Lance Armstrong. I like the race because it's a tough and dangerous event. Two years ago, there were a lot of accidents. Some cyclists were badly hurt. Last year the route was easier, so there weren't any serious accidents. I usually watch the Tour de France on TV. I'd like to go to France next year!

Lewis Tennant, Year 8

Extreme New Zealand

Reading

1 Look at the map and the photos. What are the people doing in each photo?

2 **6.9 Read about the extreme sports. Match the descriptions (1–4) with the photos (a–d).**

a

b

Culture

New Zealand

1 Tandem skydiving

You jump out of a plane at a height of 4,500 metres. You are with an experienced jump partner. You fall through the air at a speed of 200 kilometres per hour. After 60 seconds, your partner pulls the cord of the parachute. The views are fantastic!

2 Bungy jumping

You stand on the bridge across Waitemata Harbour, in Auckland. You put on a special harness, attached to a cord. You jump off the bridge and fall to the surface of the water. You touch the water for a second. The cord stops you from going into the water. It's a terrifying experience!

3 Glacier ice climbing

You are in the World Heritage Area of Fox Glacier. A helicopter takes you to the most distant part of the glacier. You take special clothes and equipment. You spend four hours on the glacier, then a helicopter takes you back to base. It's an amazing day out!

4 Canyon descent

You stand at the top of a waterfall. The river is extremely fast. You take a rope, and you climb down the waterfall. You swim through a section of water and rocks. You come to another waterfall. It's too dangerous. You walk through the forest to the bottom of the waterfall. You swim down the river. It's a real adventure!

Auckland●

●Taupo

Westland
National Park

●Wanaka

Listening

3 ⊙ 6.10 Listen to Nicky talking about her holiday in New Zealand. Which extreme sports did she try?

> bungy jumping
> canyon descent
> glacier ice climbing
> tandem skydiving

4 ⊙ 6.10 Listen again. Which extreme sport did Nicky like doing?

c

d

Biology and English
Oxygen and exercise

1 Do you know how your body uses oxygen? Read and find out.

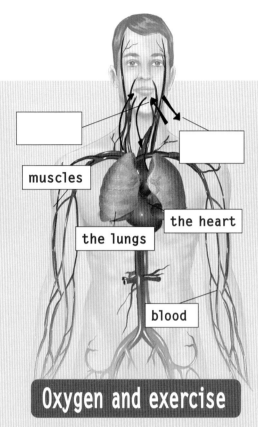

muscles

the heart

the lungs

blood

Oxygen and exercise

When we do activities like exercise and sports, we use our muscles. Muscles need oxygen to work.

We breathe oxygen into our lungs. The oxygen goes into our blood. The blood takes the oxygen into every part of the body. Our muscles use the oxygen. Our muscles make carbon dioxide. The blood takes the carbon dioxide to our lungs. We breathe carbon dioxide into the air.

When we do exercise, our muscles need a lot of oxygen. The heart works fast and it pumps the blood around the body. When we rest, the heart slows down.

2 Write *oxygen* and *carbon dioxide* in the correct boxes on the diagram.

Project

Find the pulse at your wrist. Count the beats in one minute. Now do some exercise – play a game, run or cycle. Count the beats again. Rest and wait five minutes. Count the beats again. Compare your results with the class.

Review Units 5 and 6

Vocabulary

1 Name the animals.

1 ....
2 ....
3 ....
4 ....
5 ....

1 mark per item: …/5 marks

2 Name the things.

1 ....
2 ....
3 ....
4 ....
5 ....

1 mark per item: …/5 marks

3 Write the opposites.

1 good   b..............
2 safe   d..............
3 strong   w..............
4 slow   f..............
5 scared   b..............

1 mark per item: …/5 marks

4 Write the games.

1 ....
2 ....
3 ....
4 ....
5 ....

1 mark per item: …/5 marks

5 Write the names of the food items.

1 ....
2 ....
3 ....
4 ....
5 ....

1 mark per item: …/5 marks

Grammar

6 Write true sentences with the comparative forms of the adjectives.

1 Canada / England (**big**)
2 elephants / cats (**heavy**)
3 deserts / forests (**dry**)
4 chess / draughts (**difficult**)
5 a gold medal / a silver medal (**good**)

1 mark per item: …/5 marks

7 Write the superlative form of the adjectives.

1 high
2 expensive
3 good
4 bad
5 hot

1 mark per item: …/5 marks

8 Rewrite the sentences using *must* or *mustn't*.

1 Don't take photographs here. (**take**)
2 Answer all the questions. (**answer**)
3 No outdoor shoes. (**wear**)
4 Age limit: 21 years or over. (**be**)
5 Please talk quietly. (**talk**)

1 mark per item: …/5 marks

9 Complete the sentences with *some*, *any* or *no*.

1 We had .... cake. It was delicious!
2 Did you take .... photos?
3 We didn't see .... animals.
4 There's .... food in the fridge. Let's go to the shops.
5 Let's buy .... chocolate.

1 mark per item: …/5 marks

10 Complete the sentences.

1 The Internet connection isn't fast ....
2 Some students .... have to wear uniform.
3 .... I use my dictionary in the exam?
4 You're .... young to play this game.
5 I'd like .... omelette for my lunch.

1 mark per item: …/5 marks

Communicate

11 Complete the dialogue with the sentences.

> How much is it?
> I think I'm a medium.
> Oh. Have you got a cheaper one?
> Thanks. Can I try it on?
> Yes, I'm looking for a blue T-shirt.

Assistant: Can I help you?
Jill: (1) ....
Assistant: What size are you?
Jill: (2) ....
Assistant: Here you are.
Jill: (3) ....
Assistant: Yes, of course.
Jill: (4) ....
Assistant: It's £19.95.
Jill: (5) ....
Assistant: Not at the moment, I'm afraid.
Jill: OK. Well, it's a bit too expensive. Thanks.
Assistant: OK, bye.

2 marks per item: ..../10 marks

12 Match the statements with the responses.

1 Do you have to hand this in today?
2 This is too big.
3 Can my friend come in?
4 Can we use the computer room?
5 Is it OK to talk in here?

a No, you must ask the teacher first.
b Here you are. This is smaller.
c No, you must be quiet.
d Of course she can!
e Yes, I do.

2 marks per item: ..../10 marks

13 Circle the correct sound for each word.

1	ice	/s/	/z/	6	photos	/s/	/z/
2	eyes	/s/	/z/	7	plays	/s/	/z/
3	cheese	/s/	/z/	8	price	/s/	/z/
4	chess	/s/	/z/	9	prize	/s/	/z/
5	days	/s/	/z/	10	was	/s/	/z/

1 mark per item: ..../10 marks

14 Complete the dialogue with the expressions.

> can go   can I go   you can't
> you have to   you must do

Neil: Dad, (1) .... to a concert on Tuesday?
Dad: On Tuesday? No, I'm afraid (2) ....
Neil: But Dad, it's my favourite band!
Dad: But (3) .... go to school on Wednesday.
Neil: No, I don't – Wednesday's a holiday.
Dad: Oh! Well, you (4) .... to the concert.
Neil: Thanks, Dad!
Dad: But (5) .... all your homework first.
Neil: Of course!

2 marks per item: ..../10 marks

15 Complete the report with the correct forms of the words.

> The football match on Saturday was the
> (1) .... (**good**) match of the (2) ....
> (**compete**). In fact, I think it was the (3) ....
> (**exciting**) match of the year! At the beginning,
> Liverpool were (4) .... (**good**) than Chelsea.
> The Liverpool players were (5) .... (**fast**)
> and (6) .... (**strong**) than their opponents.
> Liverpool scored two goals in the first twenty
> minutes. Chelsea weren't happy! I didn't think
> that their (7) .... (**prepare**) for the match
> was good enough. But, at half time the
> score was 2–2. The second half was (8) ....
> (**amaze**). There (9) .... (**be**) three more goals,
> and a final score of 4–3 to Chelsea! There was
> a big (10) .... (**celebrate**) in London on
> Saturday night!

1 mark per item: ..../10 marks

Total: .../100

I can...

I can buy things in shops.
I can ask for and give permission.

Reading

1 **Read the article and answer the questions.**

COUNTRY PROFILE – WALES

Wales is in the west of Great Britain. It has a population of around three million and covers an area of over 20,000 square kilometres. Its capital is Cardiff.

Weather

Temperatures are normally between zero degrees in the winter and 20 degrees in the summer, but the coldest ever was -23.3 °C in 1940. Sometimes in the winter there is a lot of snow. The highest ever was 35.2 °C in 1990. We certainly have enough rain in Wales – that's why everything is so green! So you must bring clothes to keep you warm and dry. Wales has some of the longest and most beautiful beaches in Britain, and in the summer it's usually warm enough to swim in the sea.

Animals

There aren't many wild animals in Wales, but there are a lot of cows in the fields and sheep are very popular.

Sports

There are lots of football teams in Wales but rugby is more popular here! The rules of rugby are difficult. You must run with the ball and put it down over the line to score. You can pass the ball but you mustn't throw it forwards.

1 How big is Wales?
2 How many people live there?
3 What is the capital of Wales?
4 What is the coldest it normally gets?
5 What was the coldest ever?
6 What is the hottest it normally gets?
7 What was the hottest ever?
8 Is it too cold to swim in the sea in summer?
9 What animals can you see there?
10 What is the most popular sport in Wales?

2 **Think of some information about your country. What could you say about …?**

- the weather
- animals
- popular sports

Project

Make a Country profile for your country

- Find or draw a map of your country – label the capital city
- Find out about how big your country is and how many people live there (ask someone or use the Internet)
- Write about the weather, animals and sports there
- Write about anything that makes your country different or interesting

Your body

7

> ## Grammar
Learn about the present perfect.

> ## Vocabulary
Learn words for crime, the body, and health problems.

> ## Skills
Read about a robbery, living a long healthy life, and bog bodies.

Listen to a conversation about accidents.

Write a personal letter.

> ## Communicate
Ask for and give advice.

1 Work in pairs. Look at the picture. How do you think the man feels?

2 🔘 7.1 Listen. Where are the people?
   a   at the doctor's
   b   at the hairdresser's
   c   at the dentist's

3 Work in pairs. How many parts of the body can you write in two minutes? Compare your list with a new partner.

   See Vocabulary Explorer: Page 111

4 What do you do when you don't feel well? What's the best way to feel better quickly? Tell your partner.

   See Vocabulary Explorer: Page 111

Vocabulary

1 **Work in pairs. Look at the picture. Can you see these things?**

> blood   a detective   a fingerprint   a footprint
> a hair   a murder   a robbery   a thief   a witness

See Vocabulary Explorer: Page 110

2 **Put the words in Exercise 1 into the correct group.**

1 crimes   2 evidence   3 people

Reading and listening

3 7.2 **Read and listen to the detectives' phone call. Put a tick (✓) or a cross (✗) next to the items on the Crime Scene Investigation list.**

```
Crime Scene Investigation checklist
Contact owner                          ☐
Speak to witnesses                     ☐
Photograph the scene                   ☐
Check for evidence                     ☐
Collect samples: blood                 ☐
                 hair                  ☐
Send samples to lab for DNA analysis   ☐
Take fingerprints                      ☐
```

Detective 1: I'm at Extreme Sports in the High Street. Somebody has broken the window. They've been in the shop and I think they've stolen two bikes and some sports clothes. I've contacted the owner. He's coming here now.

Detective 2: Are there any witnesses?

Detective 1: Yes, there is somebody here, but I haven't spoken to her. She's waiting outside.

Detective 2: OK. Has anybody touched anything? Remember to take some photographs of the crime scene first!

Detective 1: I've done that – I've photographed some footprints and the broken window. I've checked for evidence – there's a lot of blood on the window. I've collected a sample of the blood and a hair. Perhaps it's the thief's hair. I haven't sent the samples to the lab. And I've found something interesting! The thief has dropped an old trainer on the floor. That's very lucky for us!

Detective 2: OK, that's good. What about fingerprints?

Detective 1: Well, they've opened the safe, but they haven't taken all the money. Perhaps they've left some fingerprints on the safe door. Oh, just a minute. The owner has arrived. I have to go ... talk to you later.

Grammar: present perfect affirmative and negative

4 Look at the example. Find ten more present perfect affirmative verbs in the dialogue.

e.g. Somebody has broken the window.

5 Complete the table with *has*, *hasn't*, *have* and *haven't*.

Affirmative	
I/You/We/They He/She/It	**(1)** .... opened the safe. **(2)** .... broken the window.
Negative	
I/You/We/They He/She/It	**(3)** .... spoken to her. **(4)** .... left any fingerprints.

See Grammar Explorer: Page 126

6 Which verb in the table is regular? Find seven more regular past participles in the dialogue.

7 Complete the table with these past participles.

~~been~~	eaten	stolen	read	done	found
written	taken	had	seen	sent	given

Irregular verbs	
Infinitive	**Past participle**
be	**(1)** been
do	**(2)** ....
eat	**(3)** ....
find	**(4)** ....
give	**(5)** ....
have	**(6)** ....
read	**(7)** ....
send	**(8)** ....
steal	**(9)** ....
see	**(10)** ....
take	**(11)** ....
write	**(12)** ....

8 Complete the detective's report with the present perfect form of the verbs.

A thief (**1**) has stolen (**steal**) some sports equipment from Extreme Sports. The thief (**2**) .... (**leave**) a lot of evidence. Two witnesses (**3**) .... (**give**) information to the local police. I (**4**) .... (**take**) some photographs of the scene. At the moment, I (**5**) .... (**not finish**) my investigation because the laboratory (**6**) .... (**not look at**) the samples.

9 Complete the sentences with affirmative or negative forms of the present perfect.

e.g. My bedroom door is closed. I haven't opened (**open**) it.

1 My dad drives an old car. He .... (**buy**) a new one.

2 'Who's the letter from?' 'I don't know, I .... (**read**) it.'

3 My hair is wet. I .... (**wash**) it.

4 There is no food in the fridge. We .... (**eat**) it all!

5 I can't go out. I .... (**do**) my homework.

10 Write five sentences – four true and one false – about things you have or haven't done this week. Then work in pairs and exchange your sentences. Find your partner's false sentence.

e.g. I've eaten pizza this week.

Working with words

11 Match the words. Then complete the sentences.

1	digital		a	game
2	computer		b	phone
3	sports		c	camera
4	film		d	clothes
5	mobile		e	star

1 I can't phone you. I haven't got any credit on my ....

2 I love taking photos with my ....

3 My new .... is really difficult to play, but it's fun.

4 I wear my .... when I play football.

5 My favourite .... has won an Oscar.

Fast finishers

Look at the verb list on the inside back cover for two minutes. Then cover the column of past participles and test your memory. How did you do? Try again tomorrow and do better!

Healthy living

We spoke to three people from around the world and asked three important questions.

Have you lived a healthy life?

'Yes, I have. I've looked after myself! That's my secret and my advice to everybody. I've done a lot of exercise, I've never been lazy and I've never smoked. I haven't been ill exactly, but I've had some accidents. I'm nearly ninety, so I'm not very strong now. But I'm healthy!'

Wesley, UK

Have you ever had any illnesses?

'No, we haven't. We've sometimes been sick, but it was never serious. Just things like a cold or toothache. We've never taken any medicine for an illness. Of course, I've never drunk alcohol and James has never smoked. We haven't had a very healthy diet – we've eaten a lot of meat. These days the doctors say too much meat is bad for you. But we've been active all our lives. I'm ninety-two and I go fishing every week.'

Zelda and James, Canada

Has your grandmother ever told you her secret for a long, healthy life?

'My grandma's over eighty now, but she doesn't look it. She's never been ill. I think her secret is her diet and her personality. Firstly, she's never eaten meat. So she's had a healthy diet and she's done a lot of sport too. Secondly, she's always been a happy person. I've never seen her get angry with anybody. Her advice is always "Don't worry!"'

Sara and Kiri, New Zealand

Reading and listening

1 Work in pairs. Look at the photos. How old do you think the people are?

2 Discuss the things you should and shouldn't do to live a long life.

> be active   be happy   do sports
> eat healthy food   smoke   work hard

3 7.3 Read and listen to the interviews. What do the people talk about?

a   their jobs

b   their health

c   their families

Grammar: present perfect questions, short answers, *ever*

4 Study the table.

Questions		
Have Has	I/you/we/they he/she/it	lived a healthy life? (ever) had any illnesses?
Short answers		
Yes,	I/you/we/they he/she/it	have. has.
No,	I/you/we/they he/she/it	haven't. hasn't.

See Grammar Explorer: Page 127

5 Put the words in order to make questions.

e.g. ever / accident? / you / have / an / had
<u>Have you ever had an accident?</u>

1 been / you / lazy? / have / ever

2 you / hospital? / been / to / have

3 Zelda / any / has / medicine? / taken / ever

4 has / cigarettes? / smoked / ever / Wesley

5 had / have / you / flu?

Grammar: present perfect with *never*

6 Find these sentences in the article. Where is the correct position of *never*?

1 I've been lazy.

2 She's been ill.

See Grammar Explorer: Page 127

7 Write sentences with the present perfect and *never*.

1 she / have / toothache

2 they / take / medicine

3 you / drink / alcohol

4 I / have / a cold

5 he / eat / meat

Listening

8 Work in pairs. Think of three reasons why people go to hospital. Use your dictionary if necessary.

9 7.4 Listen to the conversation about Tommy. Tick (✓) the parts of the body the speakers mention.

ankle	arm	finger	foot
leg	neck	nose	wrist

See Vocabulary Explorer: Page 111

Vocabulary

10 Look at the pictures. Have you ever had these experiences?

1 have / toothache   2 be / in hospital

3 break / your wrist   4 sprain / your ankle

5 have / an operation   6 be / sunburnt

11 Work in groups. Ask and answer questions about the pictures in Exercise 10 with *Have you ever … ?* Then write six sentences.

e.g. <u>In my group, three people have ....</u>

See Vocabulary Explorer: Page 111

Study skills

Independent learning (1)

1 Follow these steps to improve your English.

1 Keep a record in your notebook of the mistakes you make.

2 Write three correct sentences for each mistake.

3 Next time, check your work for the mistake before you give it to the teacher.

2 Read the last writing you did. Look at spelling, grammar, word order and punctuation. Find two mistakes. Follow the steps in Exercise 1.

Doctor: Hello, Adam. Now, what's wrong with you today?

Adam: I feel terrible. I've got a sore throat and a headache.

Doctor: OK. Have you taken any medicine?

Adam: No, I haven't.

Doctor: And have you had a fever?

Adam: No, I haven't.

Doctor: Well, don't worry! I don't think you've got the flu. I think it's just a cold.

Adam: OK. What should I do?

Doctor: You should drink lots of water and take some vitamin C.

Adam: All right. Is there anything else I can do?

Doctor: Well, you can take an aspirin for your headache.

Adam: Should I stay off school for a few days? Should I stay in bed?

Doctor: No, you shouldn't. You should get lots of fresh air, so go to school as normal.

Adam: What a shame! I've got a biology exam tomorrow.

Reading and listening

1 **Look at the picture. Where is Adam?**

2 7.5 **Read and listen to the dialogue. What's the matter with Adam?**

3 **Read the dialogue again and find the doctor's advice.**

> Like all modal verbs *should* and *shouldn't* is the same for *I*, *you*, *he*, *she*, *it*, *we* and *they*.

4 7.6 **Listen and repeat the** *Useful expressions.* **Focus on your intonation.**

USEFUL EXPRESSIONS

What's wrong with you today?
I feel awful.
Don't worry.
What a shame!
What should I do?
Should I stay off school?
You should drink lots of water.
You shouldn't stay in bed.

Listening

5 7.7 **Listen to what four people said at the doctor's. Match the speakers (1–4) with the correct responses (a–e). There is one extra response.**

Speaker 1	**a**	Yes, I have.
Speaker 2	**b**	Don't worry, it's only a headache!
Speaker 3	**c**	I feel awful.
Speaker 4	**d**	You should stay in bed.
	e	No, you shouldn't stay. Stay in bed.

Speaking

6 **Work in pairs. Think of advice for these problems. Then work with a new partner. Ask for and give advice. Take turns.**

e.g. A: *What's the matter?*
    B: *I've lost my maths homework. What should I do?*
    A: *You should ….*

1 I've lost my maths homework.
2 I've had an argument with my best friend.
3 I've broken my friend's CD player.
4 My brother / sister has eaten all my chocolate.

Pronunciation: silent letters

7 7.8 **Listen to these words and look at the spelling. Underline the silent letter in each word. Then listen, check and repeat.**

answer	climb	knee	listen
right	scene	should	wrist

Writing: a personal letter

1 **Work in pairs. Read the notes (1–3) from Adam and think of advice you can give him.**

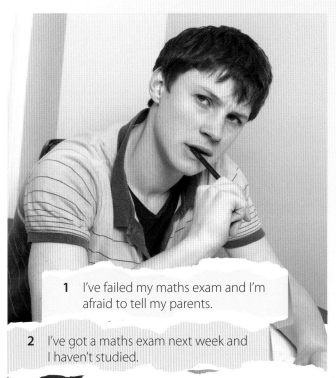

1 I've failed my maths exam and I'm afraid to tell my parents.

2 I've got a maths exam next week and I haven't studied.

3 I've passed all my exams, but my best friend has failed everything.

2 **Read the letter Adam has received from Elsa. Which note in Exercise 1 did Adam send to Elsa?**

Dear Adam,
Don't worry! It's only an exam! I think you should tell your teacher that you're worried. You should ask her for some extra help. Then you should study for half an hour every day. You can ask your friends for help too. Form a study group and work together. You shouldn't think that you're the only person with this problem. Perhaps everybody is worried! You should talk to the people in your class.
Good luck with the exam!
Best wishes,
Elsa

3 **Is Elsa's advice the same as the ideas you had in Exercise 1?**

4 **Write a reply to one of the other notes. Give advice.**

Ireland

Culture

Reading

1 Work in pairs. Look at the photos. What can you see?

2 7.9 **Read the text and answer the questions.**

1 Where is the body from?
2 How old is it?
3 Was the person rich or poor?

A few years ago, some people found a man's body in Ireland. It had long, orange hair and a broken nose. But the man wasn't a murder victim. The people didn't call the police – they called an archaeologist. The man died more than 2,300 years ago and somebody put his body in a bog. The conditions in the bog turned the man's body into a mummy. Chemicals in the bog turned his hair orange and his skin dark brown. The bog preserved the body very well. You can even see the man's fingerprints.

Bodies found in bogs are called bog bodies. The bog bodies in Ireland give us clues to how people lived and died thousands of years ago. Archaeologists examined the body. They discovered that the man had a kind of gel in his hair. This probably means the man was rich. Ordinary people didn't use cosmetics 2,300 years ago. The man was wearing a hat. The archaeologists also found some shoes and other valuable things. This was more evidence that he was not a poor man. Perhaps the man was a sacrifice to the gods. The exact details of his life, 2,300 years ago, are a mystery.

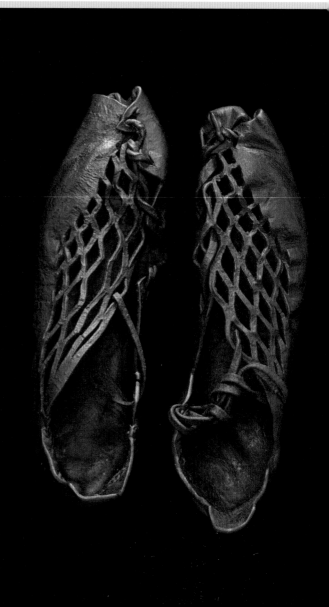

3 Read the text again and find words:

   a connected with the body.   **b** for clothes.

4 Complete the sentences with words from the text.

   1 An .... studies people and places from the past.

   2 A .... is a very wet area of land.

   3 A .... is a preserved body.

   4 People put .... on their skin or in their hair to make them more attractive.

   5 People killed animals and sometimes other people as .... for the gods.

   6 A .... is a question or problem that nobody knows the answer to.

Listening

5 7.10 **Listen to an interview with an archaeologist. Choose the correct answer.**

   1 Where was the most famous archaeological discovery?

      a Egypt   **b** England

   2 Who was Tutankhamun?

      a a farmer   **b** a king

   3 How old was he when he died?

      a eight   **b** twenty

   4 What happened to some of the archaeologists?

      a They lived long lives.   **b** They died suddenly.

Social Science and English
The European Union

1 **How much do you know about the European Union? Answer the questions in the quiz.**

Do the quiz!

1 How many countries originally formed the EU?
   a four   **b** five   **c** six

2 When did the EU start?
   a 1949   **b** 1959   **c** 1969

3 How many countries are in the EU now?
   a 22   **b** 27   **c** 30

4 How many people live in the EU?
   a 5 million **b** 51 million **c** 490 million

5 How many countries have the euro for their currency?
   a 16   **b** 19   **c** 22

6 Which country in the middle of Europe is not in the EU?
   a Belgium **b** Austria **c** Switzerland

Name the countries

Write the missing country names on the map. Use the names in the box.

Austria	Belgium	Denmark	Estonia
Finland	France	Ireland	Italy
Latvia	Lithuania	Poland	Portugal
Slovakia	Spain	Sweden	the United Kingdom

2 **Work in pairs and compare your answers. Then check your answers in the key.**

1 Sweden 2 Finland 3 Estonia 4 Latvia 5 Lithuania 6 Denmark 7 Ireland 8 the United Kingdom 9 Belgium 10 Poland 11 Slovakia 12 Austria 13 Italy 14 France 15 Spain 16 Portugal

KEY 1 c 2 a 3 b 4 c 5 a 6 c

Project

Choose a country you would like to visit. Find out about it. Prepare six multiple-choice questions about this country for other students to answer.

Exploring Africa

TRUE STORY

1 Read the text and choose the correct answer.

1 Dereck and Beverly Joubert are **married / brother and sister**.
2 They have made films about **European / African** animals.
3 Beverly's photographs have been in **magazines / advertisements**.
4 They usually get up at **4.30 / 8.30** in the morning.
5 In the summer it can be **40°C / 60°C**.
6 They believe it's good to shoot with **guns / cameras**.
7 They **often / don't often** work after dinner.
8 They have **sometimes / never** travelled outside Africa.

Dereck and Beverly Joubert

Dereck Joubert and his wife, Beverly, have made many films about wildlife in Africa. Dereck says that the animals are not just something to look at – they play an important role. Beverly thinks the wild animals can teach us a lot about ourselves. Beverly's photographs are very popular and one of them has been on the front cover of a *National Geographic* magazine.

A working day for Dereck and Beverly starts very early – at 4:30 in the morning! That's when they get up and start filming. And it's a long day – they often work until 8.30 in the evening. In the winter it's very cold and in the summer it can be 40° C. Dereck always does the filming – Beverly never does that, and she doesn't write. But Dereck never takes photographs or records the sound. They work very well as a team, and they both believe we should shoot animals with cameras – not with guns!

When they have finished filming and taking photographs for the day, they have dinner and Dereck usually writes while Beverly looks at her photographs. At night, they usually sleep in a small tent, but they sometimes sleep in the Land Cruiser – when you're very close to wild animals, it's sometimes safer to sleep in the car!

Dereck and Beverly have also travelled around the world and given talks about their work.

Films by Dereck and Beverly Joubert:
- *Eternal Enemies: Lions and Hyenas*
- *Ultimate Enemies: Elephants and Lions*
- *Relentless Enemies: Lions and Buffalo*

Books by Dereck and Beverly Joubert:
- *The Africa Diaries*
- *Hunting with the Moon*
- *The Eye of the Leopard*
- *Elephant in the Kitchen*
- *Face to Face with Lions*

2 Read the text again and answer the questions.

Who …?
films the animals
records the sound
takes photographs
gets up early in the morning
writes about the animals
says animals are more than something to look at
says we can learn from animals
sometimes sleeps in a Land Cruiser

Holidays

8

> Grammar

Learn about *will*, the first conditional, *going to*, and the present continuous for the future.

> Vocabulary

Learn words for transport, and holiday attractions.

> Skills

Read about travelling in the future, summer holidays, and school holidays in the UK.

Listen to a conversation about a holiday in Ireland.

Write a postcard.

> Communicate

Ask for tourist information, and ask for and give directions.

1 Write six words you think of when you look at the photo. Work in pairs. Compare with your partner.

2 8.1 **Listen and answer the questions.**

   1 Has the man finished his preparations?

   2 Is the girl happy with the man's preparations?

   3 What is the relationship between the two people?

   4 Who is going on holiday?

3 Work in pairs. What do you like doing on holiday? Where do you like going? Tell your partner.

See Vocabulary Explorer: Page 113

4 Work with a new partner. Compare your answers from Exercise 3. What are your two favourite things?

A family holiday – with a difference

The Branson children are looking forward to a holiday with a difference. If everything goes to plan, they will be the first family of 'space tourists'. They will travel in *SpaceShipTwo*, the first spaceship for passengers. The space travel company, Virgin Galactic, predicts that *SpaceShipTwo* will be ready to fly very soon. The flight will last about two hours but the Branson family won't be in space all of the time. It will take almost an hour to get to the edge of space – 100 kilometres above the Earth. Then the *SpaceShipTwo* passengers will be in space. They'll be weightless for about five minutes. They'll have a spectacular view of the Earth. Until now, only astronauts have seen the Earth from space. But if *SpaceShipTwo* is a success, about 5,000 space tourists a year will see the same view. A ticket for the trip will cost €100,000 per person. At the moment, about 100 people have bought tickets. Will the Branson family get a family discount on the price? It's possible – Sir Richard Branson is the owner of the Virgin Galactic!

Reading and listening

1   8.2 **Read and listen to the text about the Branson family's next holiday. Find information about these things.**

1   their destination
2   their transport
3   their travel company
4   the length of their trip
5   special tourist attractions
6   the cost of a ticket

Grammar: *will*

2   **Complete the tables with *will* and *won't*.**

Affirmative	
I/You/We/They He/She/It	(**1**) .... travel in *SpaceShipTwo*.

Negative	
I/You/We/They He/She/It	(**2**) .... be in space all of the time.

Note the abbreviations: *I will – I'll, You will – You'll, We will not – We won't,* etc.

Questions		
(3)	I/you/we/they he/she/it	get a discount?
Short answers		
Yes,	I/you/we/they he/she/it	**(4)** ....
No,	I/you/we/they he/she/it	**(5)** ....

Grammar Explorer: Page 127

3 Complete the predictions with *will* or *won't*.

e.g. The Branson family <u>will be</u> the first family of space tourists. (**be**)

1 Space tourism .... very expensive. (**be**)

2 A lot of people .... tickets for *SpaceShipTwo*. (**buy**)

3 The Earth .... different from space. (**look**)

4 Virgin Galactic .... tourists to the moon. (**not take**)

4 Write questions about the future. Then ask and answer the questions with your partner.

e.g. A: *Will space tourism be popular?*
      B: *Yes, I think it will. / No, it won't.*

1 space tourism / be popular?

2 space resorts / exist?

3 holidays on Mars / be possible?

4 people / have holidays abroad or at home?

5 air travel / be cheaper or more expensive?

5 Write predictions about the next ten years of your life. Use the ideas in the box. Compare with your partner.

e.g. <u>I think I'll be a very rich racing driver.</u>

> be a ...   buy a ...   have ... children
> live in ...   marry a ...   travel to ...
> work as a ...

Vocabulary

6 How do you travel in these vehicles – *by air, on land* or *on water*?

a balloon	....	a motorbike	....
a boat	....	a plane	....
a coach	....	a train	....
a ferry	....	a yacht	....
a helicopter	....		

See Vocabulary Explorer: Page 112

Grammar: first conditional

7 Complete the sentences from the text.

1 If everything goes to plan, they …

2 If *SpaceShipTwo* is a success, about 5,000 space tourists a year …

> Remember to use the present simple (*goes, is*) after *if*.

See Grammar Explorer: Page 127

8 Circle the correct option.

1 If we **fly** / **don't fly**, we'll get there quickly.

2 If I **go** / **don't go** by train, I'll use my travelcard.

3 If they **take** / **don't take** a taxi to the airport, they'll be late for the flight.

4 If she **takes** / **doesn't take** the ferry, she'll be seasick.

5 If he **uses** / **doesn't use** a GPS, he won't find his hotel.

9 Read the suggestions. Then complete the responses.

e.g. 'Let's leave at ten o'clock.'
    'If we <u>leave</u> (**leave**) at ten o'clock, we <u>will arrive</u> (**arrive**) on time.'

    'Let's leave at ten o'clock.'
    'If we <u>don't leave</u> (**not leave**) at ten o'clock, we <u>will</u> (**be**) late.'

1 'Let's go on holiday.'

   a 'If we .... (**go**) on holiday, I .... (**get**) a suntan.'

   b 'If we .... (**not go**) on holiday, the summer .... (**be**) boring.'

2 'Let's have a beach holiday.'

   a 'If we .... (**have**) a beach holiday, Dad .... (**not enjoy**) it.'

   b 'If we .... (**not have**) a beach holiday, Dad .... (**be**) happy.'

Fast finishers

Find six personal items.

T	I	P	P	Q	U	R	T	N	B
B	R	S	T	R	A	I	N	E	U
B	O	A	Q	E	D	I	O	U	S
E	I	A	I	P	L	A	N	E	X
V	U	Q	T	N	R	M	A	V	O
H	E	L	I	C	O	P	T	E	R
T	R	A	M	I	E	R	B	Y	M
X	I	E	C	O	A	C	H	L	R

8B Holiday plans

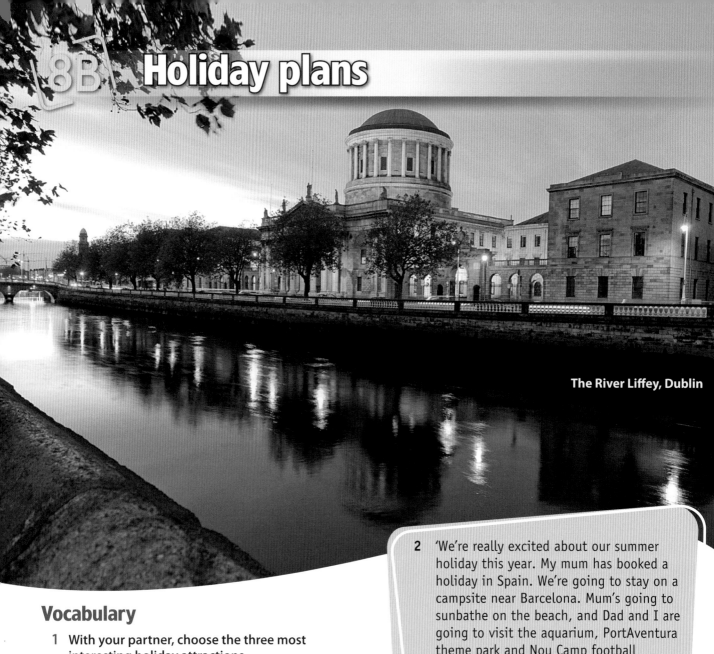

The River Liffey, Dublin

Vocabulary

1 With your partner, choose the three most interesting holiday attractions.

> an aquarium   art galleries   a beach
> a campsite   famous buildings   hotels
> museums   a swimming pool   a theme park

See Vocabulary Explorer: Page 113

Reading and listening

2 8.3 Read and listen to three people's holiday plans. Then answer the questions.

1 'I'm a train driver on the Eurostar. I've been to Paris hundreds of times, but I've never got off my train! So this summer, I'm going to have a sight-seeing holiday in Paris. I'm going to visit all the famous buildings, art galleries and museums. And I'm going to stay in a beautiful hotel next to the River Seine. I'm really looking forward to it!'

Isabel

2 'We're really excited about our summer holiday this year. My mum has booked a holiday in Spain. We're going to stay on a campsite near Barcelona. Mum's going to sunbathe on the beach, and Dad and I are going to visit the aquarium, PortAventura theme park and Nou Camp football stadium. Wow!'

Jack

3 'My cousins live in Ireland, so this summer holiday we're going to stay with them. They live near the beach but I'm not going to go swimming. The water's too cold! I'm going to look for a swimming pool. The people in their village speak Irish, so we're going to learn some expressions we can use.'

Kirsty

1 Who is going to stay with their cousins?
2 Who is going to visit a European capital city?
3 Who is going to have a family holiday abroad?

Listening

3 🔊 8.4 **Listen to Kirsty and her cousin talking about their holiday plans. Complete the calendar with the information. There is some extra information.**

> cycling along the coast   staying in a hotel
> going to the new swimming pool   visiting friends
> birthday party for Uncle Liam

JULY

Sat 21st	*driving Liverpool, ferry at 6 p.m.*
Sun 22nd	*sightseeing in Dublin*
Mon 23rd	*driving Dublin–Galway*
Tues 24th	
Wed 25th	
Thur 26th	
Fri 27th	——
Sat 28th	*home*

Grammar: *going to* and the present continuous

4 **Complete the sentences. Which sentences refer to future events? Which sentences use the present continuous?**

1 Kirsty is going to stay with her ....
2 They are going to learn some Irish ....
3 Kirsty's family is driving to Liverpool on ....
4 They are getting the ferry at ....

See Grammar Explorer: Page 127

> When we use the present continuous for future plans, we always say the date or time: *on Friday, next year, at nine o'clock tonight.*

5 **Write sentences with the present continuous.**

e.g. stay / hotel / 21st and 22nd

They are staying in a hotel on the 21st and 22nd.

1 drive / Galway / Monday
2 Uncle Liam / have a party / 24th
3 cycle / along the coast / Wednesday
4 swimming / new pool / Thursday
5 leave / 28th

6 **Write true sentences about things you have planned for the times in the box. Compare with your partner. How many things are the same?**

e.g. *I'm meeting my friends after school today.*

> after school   today   this evening   on Saturday
> on Sunday   next week   this summer

7 **Choose a holiday destination and decide what you are going to do there. Work in pairs. Ask and answer questions.**

How are you going to get to … ?
Where are you going to stay?
What are you going to do in … ?

Working with words

8 **Look at the pictures and write five sentences with the prepositions.**

e.g. Spot is .... the suitcase.

> in   near   next to   on   opposite

9 **Complete the sentences with the prepositions in Exercise 8.**

1 We're .... the train. It's leaving the station now.
2 Our campsite is .... the beach. It's about fifteen minutes' walk from here.
3 The Eiffel Tower is .... Paris.
4 Can I sit .... the window? I like looking at the scenery.
5 Our hotel is .... a hospital! We can see the people in the rooms!

8C Tourist information

Reading and listening

1   8.5 **Read and listen to the dialogue. Find the places on the map.**

Assistant: Hello, can I help you?

Kate: Yes, is the Dungeon Museum near here?

Assistant: Yes, it is. It's about five minutes from here, in the town square.

Kate: Oh, good. How do we get there?

Assistant: OK, here it is on the map. And this is the Tourist Information Centre – we're here.

Kate: Right. So we go along City Road and turn right at the end.

Assistant: No, not quite. Go along City Road and turn left at the end.

Kate: Oh yes!

Assistant: Then go along Park Road to the square. Turn right into the square. Go past the Art Gallery. The Dungeon Museum is in the corner.

Lewis: Thanks. Is there anywhere to eat near the museum?

Assistant: Yes, there's a burger bar next to it and there's a pizzeria in the opposite corner of the square.

Lewis: OK, thanks very much.

Assistant: You're welcome.

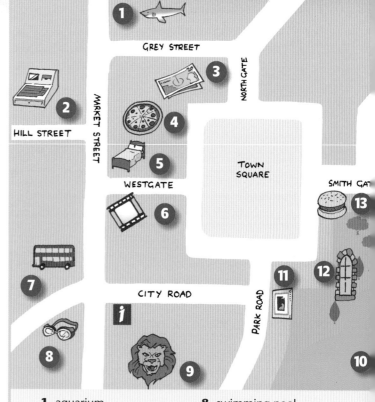

1 aquarium	8 swimming pool
2 shopping centre	9 zoo
3 bank	10 lake
4 pizzeria	11 Art Gallery
5 hotel	12 Dungeon Museum
6 cinema	13 burger bar
7 bus station	i Tourist Information

2 Find these ways of giving directions in the dialogue.

Go along + a street.
Turn left / right.
Go past + a building.
Turn into + a street, a square.

3 Cover the dialogue and look at the map. Write directions to get from the Tourist Information Centre to the Dungeon Museum. Then work in pairs. Give your directions to your partner to follow. Are they correct?

4 ☉ 8.6 Listen and repeat the *Useful expressions*. Focus on your intonation.

USEFUL EXPRESSIONS

Is the Dungeon Museum near here?
How do we get there?
Go along City Road.
Turn right. Turn Left.
Go passed the Art Gallery.
Turn right into the square.

Speaking

5 Work in pairs. You are at the Tourist Information Centre on the map. Ask your partner for directions to three places. Use the *Useful expressions*. Take turns.

e.g. A: *How do I get to the Art Gallery?*

B: *Go along …*

Writing: a postcard

1 Read Judy's postcard to Kate. Find information about these things.

1 where she is
2 what she has done
3 her plans
4 her travel plans

2 Rewrite the false sentences so that they are true. Make sure you use the underlined words.

1 It's cold and raining <u>in Barcelona</u>.
2 Judy is going to buy <u>some sunglasses</u>.
3 They haven't been to <u>the beach</u>.
4 They have been to the <u>Sagrada Família</u>.
5 They are flying <u>home</u> on Saturday.

3 Choose a holiday destination and make notes about your holiday. Use the categories in Exercise 1. Then write a postcard to a friend.

Pronunciation: syllable stress

6 ☉ 8.7 Listen and repeat the words in Groups 1 and 2. Notice which syllable is stressed.

1 ● ●●

beautiful
fashionable
gallery
interesting
passenger
wonderful

2 ●● ●

direction
enormous
expensive
gorilla
museum
successful

7 ☉ 8.8 Listen to these words. Which syllable is stressed? Listen, check and repeat.

> anything   company   exciting   explorer
> important   savannah   somebody

Hi Kate,

I can't believe we're in Barcelona! It's fantastic! The weather is wonderful and the shops are fantastic. I've bought some really cool sunglasses. We've been to the beach twice – it's right next to the city. I got sunburnt yesterday, so I'm going to visit the city today. We're going to see the Sagrada Família. We've got three more days, then we're taking the new high-speed train to Madrid on Friday. We're flying home on Sunday, so see you soon!

Love,

Judy x

UK

Culture

Reading

1　🔊 8.9 When are the school holidays in your country? Read about school holidays in the UK and find out if they are the same.

2　Read the text again and find two possible reasons why frequent school holidays are not popular.

3　Find three different types of holidays that schools can organise for their students.

What do the months of November and June have in common? They are, possibly, the only two months with no school holidays in the UK. The results of a recent survey show that frequent school holidays are not popular with everybody. In the survey, 68 per cent of 12–14 year olds said that their parents were at work in the school holidays, 73 per cent of 12–14 year olds said that they were bored during the school holidays – and 35 per cent said they were happy to go back to school!

If you don't want to stay at home and get bored, go out and try something interesting. A lot of schools organise school trips during the holidays, especially if they have a one-week holiday in October, February and May. There are a number of options.

Many schools take groups of students to outdoor centres. These trips are great for adventurous students. They also have a lot to offer students who aren't usually interested in traditional PE activities. You can do introductory courses in survival skills, for example. Students learn how to make a camp in the forest, which wild food they can eat and how to find their way back to the centre. Tree climbing, fencing and kayaking are other typical courses.

An alternative is a 'creativity' week. In most towns, there are centres which organise courses in computer game design, film making and photography. Finally, the traditional school trip abroad is always a popular option. Students can practise their foreign language skills and experience everyday life in a different culture.

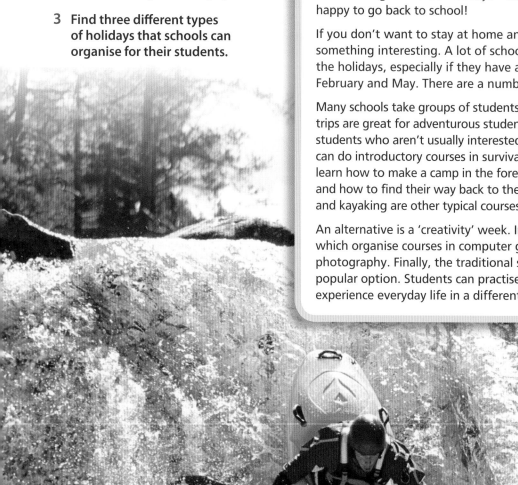

4 Read about four students. Find the best holiday for each one.

Zoe is a TV addict. She watches all the soap operas and entertains her friends with her own versions of the stories and characters.

Andy loves computer games. His ambition is to be a computer games designer, but he doesn't know very much about computer programming.

Dominic doesn't like competitive sports such as football. On the other hand, he is very athletic. He has been on a climbing wall twice and he loved it.

Cheryl's favourite subject at school is geography. When she's on trips with her family, she has an excellent sense of direction. Her family jokes that if they've got Cheryl with them, they won't need a map.

Listening

5 (8.10 **Listen to Hannah and answer the questions.**

1 When did Hannah have her holiday experience?
2 What did she do on each of the days?
3 Why is the age of sixteen important?
4 What is she going to do in her next school holiday?
5 Why does she need to find a lot of money?

Geography and English
Maps

1 How much do you know about maps? Read the text and find out.

What are maps?

Maps are representations of our world. Some maps show the features of the land around us: mountains, rivers and seas. Some maps show us how to get from one place to another. Maps can also show information about the people in different places.

Why are there different types of maps?

We need maps for different purposes. Look at the three maps (a, b and c). Which map gives the following information?

1 In which countries people speak English as an official language.
2 How to get from London to Liverpool.
3 How the River Okavango flows into the Okavango delta.

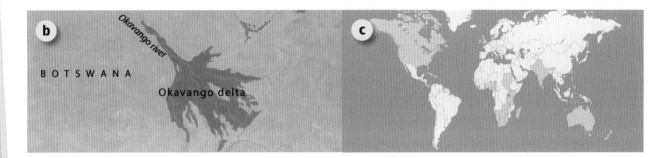

2 Work in pairs and compare your answers. Then check your answers in the key.

KEY: 1 b 2 c 3 a

Project

What can you do on holiday in your town or area? Work in groups of four. Make a poster with photos and tourist information. Present your poster to the class.

Review Units 7 and 8

Vocabulary

1 Complete the words.

1 Somebody who investigates a crime is a d............. .
2 Somebody who sees a crime is a w............. .
3 Somebody who steals things is a t............. .
4 The crime of stealing is r............. .
5 The crime of killing somebody is m............. .

1 mark per item: .../5 marks

2 Name the parts of the body.

1 ....
2 ....
3 ....
4 ....
5 ....

1 mark per item: .../5 marks

3 Write the things.

1 ....
2 ....
3 ....
4 ....
5 ....

1 mark per item: .../5 marks

4 Where can you do these things?

1 camp in a tent ....
2 see paintings ....
3 go on exciting rides ....
4 see things from the past ....
5 see animals ....

1 mark per item: .../5 marks

5 Complete the sentences with compound nouns.

1 I got a phone c............. from my cousin in France yesterday.
2 Jill wants a digital c............. .
3 You can't wear sports c............. at school.
4 Neil is playing a computer g............. .
5 The police are at the crime s............. .

1 mark per item: .../5 marks

Grammar

6 Complete the sentences with the present perfect form of the verbs.

1 I .... this magazine. (**read**)
2 Jill .... a cold. (**have**)
3 We .... dinner. (**not eat**)
4 She .... (**never smoke**)
5 He .... his arm. (**not break**)

1 mark per item: .../5 marks

7 Write present perfect questions with the words.

1 you / do / your homework?
2 they / ever / see / this film?
3 she / take / the medicine?
4 you / ever / have / an accident?
5 he / find / any evidence?

1 mark per item: .../5 marks

8 Write affirmative (✔) and negative (✗) sentences and questions (?) with *will*.

1 the train / arrive / at 6 pm (✔)
2 space travel / be / popular (?)
3 we / go / on holiday / this year (✗)
4 you / travel / by car (?)
5 the snow / stop / today (✗)

1 mark per item: .../5 marks

9 Complete the sentences.

1 If it's cold, we .... our coats. (**wear**)
2 If it rains, I .... to the beach. (**not go**)
3 If we .... late, we'll miss the bus. (**be**)
4 If he ...., he won't be seasick. (**fly**)
5 If the flights are cheap, they .... (**fly**)

1 mark per item: .../5 marks

10 Complete the sentences.

1 Big Ben is .... London.
2 My sister is .... the train now.
3 We're flying to Paris .... 21 July.
4 What are you .... to do in Paris?
5 Do I turn right or .... at the end?

1 mark per item: .../5 marks

Communicate

11 Complete the dialogue at the Tourist Information Centre with the sentences.

> Have you got a map of the town?
> How do we get there?
> OK. Is it opposite the bank?
> Yes, is the Italia Pizzeria near here?
> You're welcome.

Assistant: Can I help you?

Jill: (**1**) ....

Assistant: Yes, it's on Park Road.

Jill: (**2**) ....

Assistant: Go along Hill Street and turn right at the end.

Jill: (**3**) ....

Assistant: No, it isn't. Go past the bank and then turn right.

Jill: Hmm, I don't really understand. (**4**) ....

Assistant: Yes, here you are.

Jill: Thank you very much.

Assistant: (**5**) ....

2 marks per item: …/10 marks

12 Choose the correct response.

1 What's wrong?
   a I feel awful.
   b No, it's all right.
   c Are you OK?

2 I've got a headache.
   a Yes, I have.
   b Yes, you should.
   c You should take some medicine.

3 What should I do?
   a What a shame!
   b No, you shouldn't.
   c You should stay in bed.

4 Should I go to school?
   a No, you shouldn't.
   b You should take an aspirin.
   c Don't worry.

5 I failed my exam.
   a What's wrong?
   b What a shame!
   c Yes, you should.

2 marks per item: …/10 marks

13 Which is the silent letter in each word?

1	answer	6	island
2	climb	7	science
3	listen	8	half
4	should	9	know
5	wrist	10	wrong

1 mark per item: …/10 marks

14 Which syllable is stressed in each word?

1	anything	6	important
2	exciting	7	museum
3	explorer	8	possible
4	gorilla	9	vegetable
5	holiday	10	wonderful

1 mark per item: …/10 marks

15 Complete the postcard with the words in the box.

> at   has   in   near   on   so
> some   to   to   will

Hi Neil,

I can't believe we're (**1**) .... Egypt! It's fantastic! I've seen (**2**) .... amazing things. We've been (**3**) .... the desert today and we're going (**4**) .... go shopping tomorrow! Our hotel is great – it's (**5**) .... the river. Dad (**6**) .... been here before, (**7**) .... he knows a lot of good places. He's booked a trip on the river – I think it (**8**) .... be beautiful! We're flying home (**9**) .... Sunday. Are you coming to meet us (**10**) .... the airport?

Love,

Jill x

1 mark per item: …/10 marks

Total: …/100

I can...

I can ask for and give advice.

I can ask for tourist information.

I can ask for and give directions.

Free-time interests and activities

1 animals
2 cycling
3 dancing
4 doing homework
5 doing housework
6 drawing
7 fashion
8 going to the cinema
9 meeting friends
10 music
11 painting
12 playing the drums
13 playing football
14 playing computer games
15 reading
16 singing
17 skateboarding
18 sports
19 studying
20 swimming
21 taking photos
22 tidying my bedroom
23 watching TV

1 VE1 **Listen and repeat.**

2 VE2 **Cover the word box. Listen and say the number.**

3 **Work in pairs.**

   A: Say a number.
   B: Cover the word box. Say the activity.

   Take turns.

   e.g. **A:** *12*
       B: *playing the drums*

Performing

1. act in a film
2. act in a play
3. dance in a show
4. do magic
5. perform in a circus
6. play an instrument
7. play in a band
8. sing in a concert
9. take part in a festival
10. wear a costume
11. wear make up

1.  VE3 **Listen and repeat.**

2. VE4 **Cover the word box. Listen and say the number.**

3. **Work in pairs.**

   A: Say an activity.
   B: Cover the word box. Say the number.

   Take turns.

   e.g. **A:** *dance in a show*
   B: *3*

Weather

1 cloudy
2 cold
3 foggy
4 hot
5 icy
6 raining
7 snowing
8 stormy
9 sunny
10 windy
11 lightning
12 a hurricane
13 a tornado
14 a tsunami
15 a snowstorm

1 VE5 **Listen and repeat.**

2 VE6 **Cover the word box. Listen and say the number.**

3 **Work in pairs.**

A: Say a number.
B: Cover the word box. Say the weather word.

Take turns.

e.g. A: *7*
B: *snowing*

Jobs

1	a builder
2	a dentist
3	a doctor
4	a factory worker
5	a farmer
6	a fire fighter
7	a nurse
8	an office worker
9	a pilot
10	a police officer
11	a receptionist
12	a reporter
13	a scientist
14	a shop assistant
15	a singer
16	a teacher
17	a truck driver
18	a vet
19	a waiter
20	a writer

1 VE7 **Listen and repeat.**

2 VE8 **Cover the word box. Listen and say the number.**

3 **Work in pairs.**

   A: Say a job.
   B: Cover the word box. Say the number.

   Take turns.

   e.g. A: *a doctor*
   B: *3*

Mass media

1 a blog
2 a book
3 a CD
4 a DVD
5 an email
6 a film
7 the Internet
8 a magazine
9 a newspaper
10 a podcast
11 a radio programme
12 a text message
13 a TV programme

1 VE9 **Listen and repeat.**

2 VE10 **Cover the word box. Listen and say the number.**

3 **Work in pairs.**

A: Say a number.
B: Cover the word box. Say the media word.

Take turns.

e.g. A: *7*
B: *the Internet*

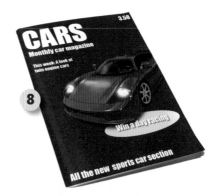

Films

1 an action film
2 a cartoon
3 a comedy
4 a fantasy film
5 a horror film
6 a musical
7 a romance
8 a science fiction film

1 ◉VE11 **Listen and repeat.**

2 ◉VE12 **Cover the word box. Listen and say the number.**

3 **Work in pairs.**

A: Say a film.

B: Cover the word box. Say the number.

Take turns.

e.g. A: *a horror film*

B: *5*

TV programmes

1 a chat show
2 a documentary
3 a drama
4 a game show
5 the news
6 a quiz show
7 a reality TV show
8 a soap opera

1 ◉VE13 **Listen and repeat.**

2 ◉VE14 **Cover the word box. Listen and say the word.**

3 **Work in pairs.**

A: Say a number.

B: Cover the word box. Say the TV programme.

Take turns.

e.g. A: *6*

B: *a quiz show*

Life events

1. be born
2. go to school
3. grow up
4. leave school
5. go to university
6. pass an exam
7. graduate from university
8. get a job
9. become a teacher
10. get married
11. have a family

1. VE15 **Listen and repeat.**

2. VE16 **Cover the word box. Listen and say the number.**

3. **Work in pairs.**

   A: Say a life event.
   B: Cover the word box. Say the number.

   Take turns.

   e.g. A: *leave school*
   B: *4*

Appearance

1. old
2. young
3. short
4. tall
5. fat
6. slim
7. black hair
8. blond hair
9. dark hair
10. fair hair
11. red hair
12. long hair
13. short hair
14. curly hair
15. straight hair
16. wavy hair
17. blue eyes
18. brown eyes
19. a beard
20. a moustache
21. a scar
22. a tattoo

1. ⊙VE17 **Listen and repeat.**

2. ⊙VE18 **Cover the word box. Listen and say the number.**

3. **Work in pairs.**

   A: Say a number.
   B: Cover the word box. Say the appearance word.

   Take turns.

   e.g. A: *12*
   B: *long hair*

Animals

1	an ant
2	an antelope
3	a bear
4	a cat
5	a cheetah
6	a cow
7	a crocodile
8	a dog
9	an elephant
10	a giraffe
11	a gorilla
12	a hamster
13	a hippopotamus
14	a lion
15	a mouse
16	a rabbit
17	a shark
18	a snake
19	a tortoise
20	a whale
21	a zebra

1 VE19 **Listen and repeat.**

2 VE20 **Cover the word box. Listen and say the number.**

3 **Work in pairs.**

A: Say an animal.

B: Cover the word box. Say the number.

Take turns.

e.g. **A:** *a rabbit*
　　 B: *16*

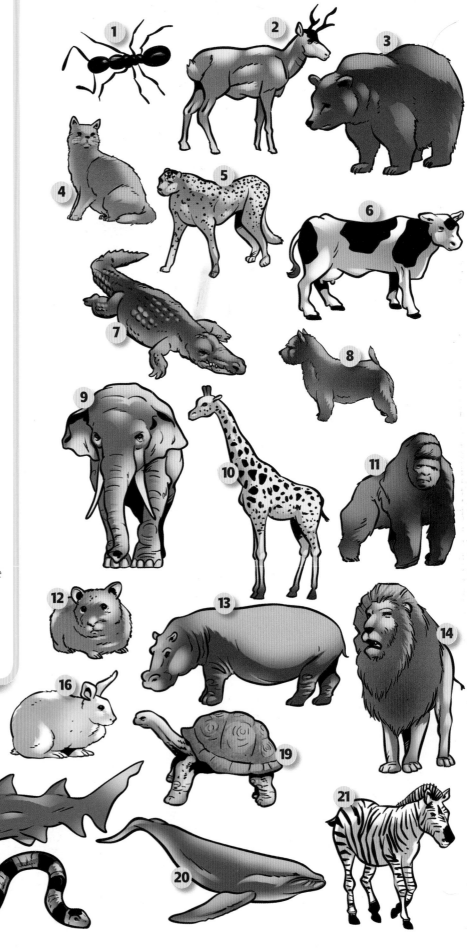

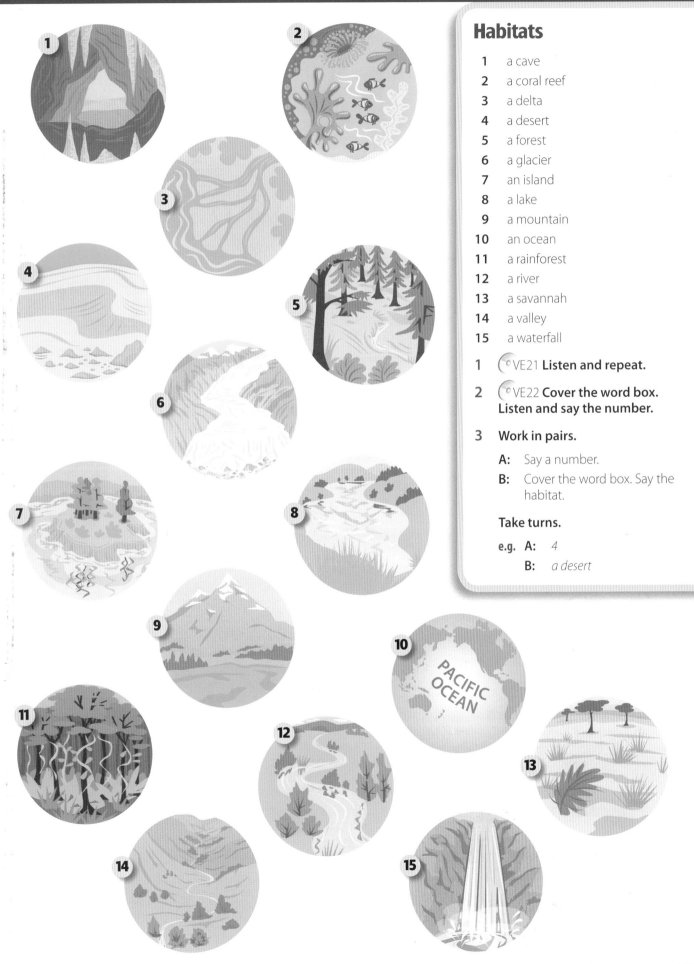

Habitats

1 a cave
2 a coral reef
3 a delta
4 a desert
5 a forest
6 a glacier
7 an island
8 a lake
9 a mountain
10 an ocean
11 a rainforest
12 a river
13 a savannah
14 a valley
15 a waterfall

1 VE21 **Listen and repeat.**

2 VE22 **Cover the word box. Listen and say the number.**

3 **Work in pairs.**

A: Say a number.

B: Cover the word box. Say the habitat.

Take turns.

e.g. **A:** *4*

B: *a desert*

Sports and games

1	badminton
2	baseball
3	basketball
4	bowling
5	cards
6	chess
7	computer games
8	cricket
9	darts
10	dominoes
11	draughts
12	football
13	golf
14	handball
15	hockey
16	rugby
17	squash
18	table tennis
19	tennis
20	volleyball

1   VE23 **Listen and repeat.**

2   VE24 **Cover the word box. Listen and say the number.**

3   **Work in pairs.**

   A: Say a sport or game.

   B: Cover the word box. Say the number.

   Take turns.

   e.g.   **A:**   *football*

         B: *12*

Food

1 beans
2 biscuits
3 cereal
4 cheese
5 chocolate
6 coffee
7 crisps
8 eggs
9 fish
10 fruit
11 jam
12 juice
13 lemonade
14 milk
15 oil
16 an omelette
17 pasta
18 rice
19 sugar
20 tea
21 vegetables
22 yoghurt

1 ○VE25 **Listen and repeat.**

2 ○VE26 **Cover the word box. Listen and say the number.**

3 **Work in pairs.**

   A: Say a number.

   B: Cover the word box. Say the food item.

Take turns.

  e.g. A: *5*

      B: *chocolate*

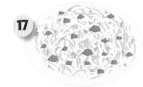

Crime

1. an alarm
2. blood
3. a crime scene
4. a detective
5. evidence
6. a fingerprint
7. a footprint
8. a hair
9. a murder
10. the police
11. a robbery
12. a safe
13. a sample
14. a thief
15. a witness

1. VE27 **Listen and repeat.**

2. VE28 **Cover the word box. Listen and say the number.**

3. **Work in pairs.**

   A: Say a word.
   B: Cover the word box. Say the number.

   Take turns.

   e.g. **A:** *a sample*
       B: *13*

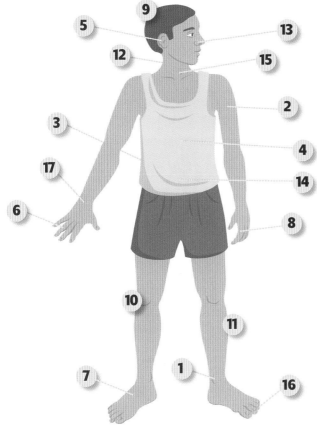

Parts of the body

1	ankle	10	knee
2	arm	11	leg
3	back	12	neck
4	chest	13	nose
5	ear	14	stomach
6	finger	15	throat
7	foot	16	toe
8	hand	17	wrist
9	head		

1 🔊VE29 **Listen and repeat.**

2 🔊VE30 **Cover the word box. Listen and say the number.**

3 **Work in pairs.**

A: Say a number.

B: Cover the word box. Say a part of the body.

Take turns.

e.g. **A:** *6*

B: *finger*

Health problems

1	a broken arm
2	a cold
3	a cough
4	earache
5	a fever
6	the flu
7	a headache
8	a sore throat
9	a sprained ankle
10	sunburn
11	toothache

1 🔊VE31 **Listen and repeat.**

2 🔊VE32 **Cover the word box. Listen and say the number.**

3 **Work in pairs.**

A: Say a health problem.

B: Cover the word box. Say the number.

Take turns.

e.g. **A:** *a cold*

B: *2*

Transport

1	a balloon
2	a bike
3	a boat
4	a bus
5	a car
6	a coach
7	a ferry
8	a helicopter
9	a motorbike
10	a plane
11	a spaceship
12	a taxi
13	a train
14	a tram
15	the underground
16	a yacht

1 VE33 **Listen and repeat.**

2 VE34 **Cover the word box.
   Listen and say the number.**

3 **Work in pairs.**

   A: Say a number.
   B: Cover the word box. Say the
   transport word.

   Take turns.

   e.g. **A:** *5*
   　　 B: *a car*

Holiday attractions

1	an aquarium
2	an art gallery
3	a beach
4	a burger bar
5	a café
6	a campsite
7	a church
8	a hotel
9	a museum
10	an outdoor activity centre
11	a park
12	a pizzeria
13	a restaurant
14	a shop
15	a shopping centre
16	a stadium
17	a swimming pool
18	a theme park
19	a zoo

1 VE35 **Listen and repeat.**

2 VE36 **Cover the word box. Listen and say the number.**

3 **Work in pairs.**

A: Say a holiday attraction.
B: Cover the word box. Say the number.

Take turns.

e.g. **A:** *a restaurant*
B: *13*

1 Steel drums

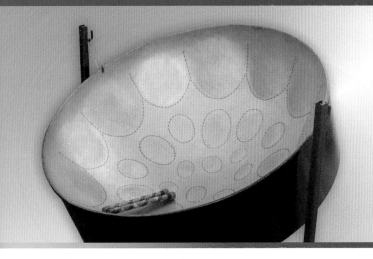

Steelband music, or pan, was invented on the Caribbean islands of Trinidad and Tobago. The music originally comes from Africa. People who came to the islands from Africa played the rhythms of their music by beating on old steel oil drums. Now, the sound of steelband is an important part of island culture.

Before you watch

1 You are going to watch a film about steelband music. What different instruments are you going to hear? Make a list. Watch and see if you are right.

While you watch

PART ONE: This is steelband music

2 **Listen and repeat these words.**

> important   invented   home

Now watch the first part of the film and write the words in the gaps.

1 Trinidad and Tobago is the .... of steelband or 'pan' music.

2 Steelband music is a(n) .... part of the culture of the islands.

3 Pan is the only musical instrument that was .... in the 20th century.

PART TWO: A history of steelband

3 **Listen and repeat these words.**

> oil   ear   sound   rhythms

Now watch the second part of the film and put these words in the gaps.

1 The drums produce a(n) .... which has influenced the music of the region.

2 The big steel drums once contained ....

3 The .... come from Africa.

4 People don't follow music on paper; they play by ....

PART THREE: Sharing steelband music

4 **Listen and repeat these words.**

> panyards   performers   tuner

Now watch the third part of the film and write the words in the gaps.

1 The person who tunes the drums is the ....

2 These instruments are used by some of the islands' top ....

3 Every night, places called .... are full of people who come to learn to play.

After you watch

5 **Read the introduction again and watch the whole film. Are the sentences true (T) or false (F)?**

1 The islands in the Caribbean region are famous for their lively music.   **T / F**

2 Many Caribbean islands are home to steelband music.   **T / F**

3 The early Africans used their own drums.   **T / F**

4 Steelband musicians usually play by ear.   **T / F**

5 It is easy to tune the drums.   **T / F**

6 **Put the words in the correct order to make questions for the answers in bold.**

Q islands / from? / does / steelband / Which / music / come   **Trinidad and Tobago.**

....

Q is / called? / tuner / What   **The Honey boy.**

....

Q do / rhythms / of / music / the / come / originally / Where / from? / the   **Africa.**

....

Q go / people / do / play / drums? / the / Where / learn / to / to   **Panyards.**

....

2 Volcano trek

Erta Ale is a live volcano in a remote region of Ethiopia. A group of explorers and two geologists from the University of Nice have travelled to the volcano. The oldest lava lake in the world is at the bottom of the crater. The geologists collect samples of the red hot lava. They will study these samples to help them understand how the Earth began millions of years ago.

Before you watch

1 **You are going to watch a film about a volcano in Ethiopia. Label the diagram with these words.**

> crater   lava   magma

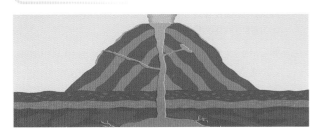

While you watch

PART ONE: The Erta Ale volcano

2 **Listen and repeat these words.**

> crater   lava   temperature   camels

Now watch the first part of the film and write the words in the gaps.

1 Hot .... has erupted from the volcano for 100 years.
2 The .... of this lava is 2,000 degrees Fahrenheit.
3 The team has travelled on .... to reach the volcano.
4 The black lava lake is deep in the ....

PART TWO: How volcanoes work

3 **Listen and repeat these words.**

> plates   geologists   lake

Now watch the second part of the film and put these words in the gaps.

1 The continental .... move farther apart every year.

2 The .... is one of the lowest points on Earth.
3 The .... are studying how the world started millions of years ago.

PART THREE: Entering the volcano

4 **Listen and repeat these words.**

> samples   morning   smell   analyse

Now watch the third part of the film and write the words in the gaps.

1 Even in the early .... , it's very, very hot.
2 There is a strong .... of sulphur.
3 Professor Tessier wants to collect .... of the red hot lava.
4 The team will go back to .... the samples.

After you watch

5 **Read the introduction again and watch the whole film. Are the sentences true (T) or false (F)?**

1 The temperature of the lava is more than 1,000 degrees Fahrenheit.   T / F
2 Franck Tessier and Irene Margaritis are geophysicists at the University of Nice.   T / F
3 The Erta Ale volcano has the biggest lava lake in the world.   T / F
4 As the lava cools down, it becomes hard and black.   T / F
5 In the crater, it is very hot and there is a strong smell of sulphur.   T / F
6 The team returns from the crater at four o'clock in the morning.   T / F
7 The pieces of lava the team collect are not directly from the lava lake.   T / F

Wildfire photographer

Mark Thiessen spends his summer holidays taking photographs of wildfires. He takes photographs for his job as a photographer with National Geographic, but he has loved chasing the fires since he was a small boy. The fires are dangerous but beautiful. Mark loves photographing them because he never knows what will happen next. He also photographs fire fighters and works with them as part of their team.

Before you watch

1 You are going to watch a film about a man who photographs fires. Which three adjectives below could you use to describe a fire?

> exciting   safe   normal
> dangerous   hot   boring

While you watch

PART ONE: The photographer

2 Listen and repeat these words.

> wildfires   senses   exciting

Now watch the first part of the film and write the words in the gaps.

1 Mark's job as a photographer is not as .... as people think.

2 When you are photographing a fire, all your .... come alive.

3 Instead of running after wild animals, Mark runs after ....

PART TWO: The fire

3 Listen and repeat these words.

> tornado   desert   happen

Now watch the second part of the film and put these words in the gaps.

1 Mark rides through a huge fire that is spreading across the Idaho ....

2 You never know what's going to .... next.

3 A fire .... can be up to ten metres high.

PART THREE: Working with the fire fighters

4 Listen and repeat these words.

> fire fighters   beautiful   destroy   goal

Now watch the third part of the film and write the words in the gaps.

1 His .... is to photograph the men and women who fight the fires.

2 When Mark is with the .... , he feels part of a team.

3 Fires can .... a lot of land.

4 Trees damaged by fire can be quite ....

After you watch

5 Read the introduction and watch the whole film. Are the sentences true (T) or false (F)?

1 Mark spends his holidays photographing fires. **T / F**

2 His job as a National Geographic photographer is exciting. **T / F**

3 There is a big fire spreading across the desert. **T / F**

4 Mark is also a fire fighter. **T / F**

6 Watch the film again. Put the words and phrases in the correct order to make sentences.

1 when you're / come alive / your / photographing / a fire. / senses / All of

....

2 animals. / photograph / things like / dangerous / wild / He doesn't

....

3 and / drives west. / So, every summer, / his / photographic / Mark takes / equipment

....

4 tornado / It's like a / going across / the truck. / the front of

....

4 Taiko master

Taiko drumming started in Japan two thousand years ago. Taiko Master Seiichi Tanaka came to San Francisco from Japan in 1968 and he began to make Taiko popular in America. The essence of Taiko is unity of the drummers and the energy they create. Because of Seiichi Tanaka, there are lots of Taiko groups in San Francisco and all over America.

Before you watch

1   You are going to watch a film about a Japanese art/sport called Taiko. What other things do you know that come from Japan? Make a list.

While you watch

PART ONE: Where Taiko began

2   Listen and repeat these words.

> sound   drummers   audience

Now watch the first part of the film and write the words in the gaps.

1   In the United States, a new .... is listening to this ancient drum.
2   The essence of Taiko is the unity of the .... amongst themselves.
3   It's an art form that brings together .... , body and mind.

PART TWO: A history of Taiko in the USA

3   Listen and repeat these words .

> groups   energy   style

Now watch the second part of the film and write the words in the gaps.

1   Seiichi Tanaka arrived and brought a new .... of drumming.
2   There are now about 800 .... spread all over this country and Canada.
3   The .... from Mother Nature goes through your body into the drumstick.

PART THREE: Modern Taiko

4   Listen and repeat these words.

> express   pain   excitement

Now watch the third part of the film and write the words in the gaps.

1   The drummers have to play through .... and tiredness.
2   At that point, drummers feel they can .... their feelings and energy.
3   North America has the chance to enjoy the energy and .... of modern Taiko.

After you watch

5   Read the introduction again and watch the whole film. Are the sentences true (T) or false (F)?

1   Taiko comes from San Francisco.   T / F
2   Taiko is 2,000 years old.   T / F
3   Seiichi Tanaka arrived in Japan in 1968.   T / F
4   There aren't many Taiko groups in America now.   T / F
5   In Taiko, you have to give 110 per cent.   T / F

6   Match the questions (1–5) with the answers (a–e).

1   Which country is Taiko from?
2   Which city in the USA did Seiichi Tanaka come to live in?
3   How many Taiko groups are there now in the USA and Canada?
4   What does modern Taiko bring together?
5   How old is Taiko?

a   Sound, body and mind.
b   San Francisco.
c   Japan.
d   800.
e   2,000 years old.

5 A disappearing world

Dr Fay is making a journey through the Congo rainforest in Africa. It is very big and you can find almost half of the plants and wildlife that exist in Africa here. He is recording all the animals, trees and plants he finds before they disappear forever. After eight months, the team are in Gabon. They have to climb some hills and then they cross the rapids of a dangerous river.

Before you watch

1 You are going to watch a film about an expedition in the Congo. Which of these words are connected to water – and which to land?

> rapids   stepping stones   rainforest
> river   hill   trees

While you watch

PART ONE: A desperate expedition

2 Listen and repeat these words.

> record   scientist   expedition

Now watch the first part of the film and write the words in the gaps.

1 In the Congo, just north of the equator, a special .... is beginning.

2 Their aim is to make a scientific .... of a world which is disappearing.

3 Doctor Michael Fay is a(n) ....

PART TWO: The rainforest

3 Listen and repeat these words.

> hills   humans   half

Now watch the second part of the film and write the words in the gaps.

1 The rainforest may have .... of all of the wild plants and animals found in Africa.

2 At last, the men reach the .... and begin to walk up.

3 There are no .... ; there's not a single village or road.

PART THREE: The rapids

4 Listen and repeat these words.

> landscape   forests   challenge

Now watch the third part of the film and write the words in the gaps.

1 The team can hear their next .... before they see it.

2 The Kongou Chutes are an important part of the .... the team wants to protect.

3 This land of old fast water and old .... is in danger because of logging.

After you watch

5 Read the introduction again and watch the whole film. Are the sentences true (T) or false (F)?

1 The expedition begins in December.   T / F

2 Dr Fay thinks that if they do not document everything now, there may not be another chance.   T / F

3 He wants to document the humans, the plants and the animals that he sees.   T / F

4 In Gabon they climb strange hills made of stone.   T / F

5 The old forests are in danger because of logging.   T / F

6 The team uses a guide to help them get across the river.   T / F

7 Dr Fay's expedition lasts one year.   T / F

6 Greek olives

Olives are important for the island of Naxos and everywhere in the Mediterranean. The olive branch has been a symbol of peace since ancient times. People use every part of the olive tree, but a lot of olives are used for oil. The best liquid comes from olives picked as soon as they become black; the oil is used for many things, including food, light and medicine.

Before you watch

1 You are going to watch a film about Greek olives. Which three words go with the word 'olive'?

> oil   car   island   tree   drink   branch

While you watch

PART ONE: The colour of olives

2 Listen and repeat these words.

> same   Mediterranean   collect

Now watch the first part of the film and write the words in the gaps.

1 Olives are very important in the ....
2 Green and black olives come from the .... tree.
3 To have green olives, you .... them when they are young.

PART TWO: The taste of olives

3 Listen and repeat these words.

> goddess   thousands   branch

Now watch the second part of the film and write the words in the gaps.

1 Some olive trees are .... of years old.
2 The olive .... is a sign of peace.
3 Eirene is the .... of peace.

PART THREE: The uses of olives

4 Listen and repeat these words.

> medicine   peace   vitamins

Now watch the third part of the film and write the words in the gaps.

1 The oil is used for cooking, for light and sometimes as ....
2 Olives also contain lots of ....
3 Olive trees give a feeling of ....

After you watch

5 Read the introduction again and watch the whole film. Are the sentences true (T) or false (F)?

1 Olives are important in most of the Mediterranean. **T / F**
2 Green and black olives don't come from the same tree. **T / F**
3 Without the fruit, the olive tree is not easy to identify. **T / F**
4 Everybody loves olives. **T / F**
5 In Greek history, the goddess of peace carries an olive leaf. **T / F**
6 Olive oil is healthy and full of vitamins. **T / F**

6 Watch the film again. Put the words and phrases in the correct order to make sentences.

1 people / probably / recognise / olive tree. / wouldn't / an / Most

   ....

2 alive / been / thousands of / years. / Some / have / olive trees / for

   ....

3 olive oil. / Many / of the / produced in / used for / olives / Greece / are

   ....

4 can / every part / use / You / tree. / olive / of the

   ....

7 Farley the red panda

Farley is a red panda born in a zoo in San Diego. His mother couldn't look after him. The people at the zoo started to raise him by hand, but when he was three weeks old he got very ill. He was in hospital for a long time, but he got better. Then he was moved to a zoo in New York. There is another panda the same age for him to play with there and he is doing very well.

Before you watch

1   You are going to watch a film about a red panda called Farley who spends a lot of time in hospital. Match the words with the definitions.

> x-ray   injection   to   tube   feed

1   liquid put into the body using a needle
2   a photograph to show the inside of your body
3   to give food in a liquid through a plastic tube

While you watch

PART ONE: Meet Farley

2   Listen and repeat these words.

> infection   temperature   medicine

Now watch the first part of the film and write the words in the gaps.

1   When they found him, he had a very low body ....
2   When he was about three weeks old, he got a bad ....
3   With .... and lots of care, he got better.

PART TWO: Farley's future

3   Listen and repeat these words.

> surprise   hospital   keepers

Now watch the second part of the film and write the words in the gaps.

1   After he was in hospital for a time, the .... began to wonder, 'Is Farley happy?'
2   After a long stay in .... , Farley was ready to go home.
3   Farley has another .... coming up.

PART THREE : A new life

4   Listen and repeat these words.

> company   fighter   playmates

Now watch the third part of the film and write the words in the gaps.

1   It is important for young pandas to have ....
2   They really like each other's .... , and they like to play and sleep together.
3   Farley was special because he was a ....

After you watch

5   Read the introduction again and watch the whole film. Put the events in the correct order (1–6).

.... He moves back to the nursery.
.... He is very ill and goes to hospital.
.... He bonds with Banshee.
.... He learns to climb and go exploring.
.... The zoo keepers find Farley, cold and hungry.
.... He travels to the zoo in Syracuse, New York.

6   Watch the film again. Put the words and phrases in the correct order to make sentences.

1   much / The nursery workers / didn't have / raising / by hand. / red pandas / experience of
   ....

2   With / he slowly / got better. / and lots of care, / medicine
   ....

3   pleased with / Soon, / improvement. / everyone was / Farley's
   ....

4   was special / She explains that / because he was / Farley / fighter. / such a
   ....

120

8 Living in Venice

Early in the morning is the only time that the people of Venice have the city to themselves. The rest of the time, the city is full of tourists. The crowds of tourists can cause problems for the people who live in Venice. The city has become very expensive. If you don't want to work in tourism, there aren't many other jobs. Many young people are leaving, but those people who stay really love the city.

Before you watch

1 You are going to watch a film about tourism in the city of Venice. Match the words with the definitions.

> crowds   piazza   gondola   canal

1 a type of boat
2 a type of river, but man-made
3 a large group of people
4 a square in an Italian city

While you watch

PART ONE: Morning in Venice

2 Listen and repeat these words.

> crowds   quality   market

Now watch the first part of the film and write the words in the gaps.

1 In the Piazza San Marco, the traders are getting ready for the .... of visitors.
2 Early morning is the best time for shopping in the ....
3 Venice is a city that is clean and easy to live in, with a high .... of life.

PART TWO: Living in Venice

3 Listen and repeat these words.

> property   work   population

Now watch the second part of the film and write the words in the gaps.

1 The .... of Venice is getting older.
2 .... is particularly expensive.

3 The huge crowds of visitors make getting home from .... very difficult.

PART THREE: Working in Venice

4 Listen and repeat these words.

> cities   living   challenges

Now watch the third part of the film and write the words in the gaps.

1 It can be difficult to earn a .... here.
2 Other .... are not very different.
3 Despite all the .... , it's difficult to think of living anywhere else.

After you watch

5 Read the introduction again and watch the whole film. Are the sentences true (T) or false (F)?

1 It is early evening in Venice.   T / F
2 In a few hours, hundreds of people will come to the square.   T / F
3 The population of Venice isn't getting younger.   T / F
4 Other big cities are less expensive than Venice.   T / F
5 People say that anyone who comes to Venice will fall in love.   T / F

6 Answer the questions. Watch the film again to check your answers.

1 When do the people of Venice have the city to themselves?
2 What are the three positive reasons for living in Venice?
3 Why is it difficult for young people to find somewhere to live?
4 Which century does the city feel like?
5 In Venice, who can you always fall in love with?

Grammar Explorer

Starter Unit

be, have got

The present simple of **be** has three forms: **am**, **are** and **is**.
I am a boy.   *You/We/They are students.*   *He/She/It is old.*

Affirmative		
I'm	You're/We're/They're He's/She's/It's	at school.
Negative		
I'm not	You/We/They aren't He/She/It isn't	at school.
Questions		
Am Are Is	I you/we/they he/she/it	at school?
Short answers		

Yes,	I am. you/we/they are. he/she/it is.	No,	I'm not. you/we/they aren't. he/she/it isn't.

The present simple of **have got** has two forms: **have got** and **has got**.
I/You/We/They have got lots of friends.
He/She/It has got long legs.

Affirmative		
I/You/We/They He/She/It	've got 's got	a new book.
Negative		
I/You/We/They He/She/It	haven't got hasn't got	a new book.
Questions		
Have Has	I/you/we/they he/she/it	got	a new book?
Short answers				

Yes,	I/you/we/they he/she/it	have. has.	No,	I/you/we/they he/she/it	haven't. hasn't.

there is/are

We use **there is** (singular) and **there are** (plural) to describe what is in a place. In the affirmative, we use **some** with nouns in the plural.
There is a teacher's desk in the classroom.
There are some posters on the walls.

Affirmative			
There's There are	a some	book books	on the table.
Negative			
There isn't There aren't	a any	book books	on the table.
Questions			
Is there Are there	a any	book books	on the table?
Short answers			

Yes, there is. Yes, there are.	No, there isn't. No, there aren't.

can

We use **can** to talk or ask about ability. **Can** has the same form for all subjects (*I, you, he*, etc). The main verb after **can** is in the **bare infinitive**.
She can sing very well.   *Can you speak Italian?*

Affirmative	
I/You/We/They/He/She/It	can swim.
Negative	
I/You/We/They/He/She/It	can't (cannot) swim.
Question		
Can	I/you/we/they/he/she/it	swim?
Short answers		
Yes, No,	I/you/we/they/he/she/it I/you/we/they/he/she/it	can. can't.

s – is, has or possessive

An apostrophe (**'s**) is used in the short form of **present continuous** and **has got**, as well as for **possessives**.
John's looking at you. (**is** *looking* – present continuous)
John's got lots of friends. (**has** *got*)
John's best friend is really nice. (possessive)

possessive adjectives

We use a **possessive adjective** before a noun to say who/what it belongs to or is related to.
I like school. My favourite subject is maths.
She's my grandmother. Her son is my dad.
They're my friends. This is their house.

Subject pronouns							
I	you	he	she	it	we	you	they
Possessive adjectives							
my	your	his	her	its	our	your	their

Unit 1
present simple

We use **present simple** to talk about things that are always true, things we do often or that happen often, etc.
It snows in winter.
My cousin lives in London.
I watch TV every evening.

In the affirmative, we add **-s** to the verb after *he*, *she* or *it*.
I/You/We/They **like music.**   *He/She/It* **likes sports.**

> With verbs ending in **-ss**, **-sh**, **-ch**, **-x** and **-o**, we add **-es**.
> mi**ss**es   wa**sh**es   wat**ch**es   fi**x**es   g**o**es
> With verbs ending in a **consonant + -y**, we change the **-y** to **-ies**.
> stu**dy**   studies   car**ry**   carries

In the negative, we use **don't** or **doesn't** and the bare infinitive of the main verb. We DON'T add **–s** or **–es** to the main verb.
I don't like *history.*
Kate doesn't speak *Italian.*

Affirmative		
I/You/We/They He/She/It	love loves	skateboarding.
Negative		
I/You/We/They He/She/It	don't (do not) doesn't (does not)	play the violin. like a lot of noise.

adverbs of frequency

We use **adverbs of frequency** to talk about habits or how often something happens.

100% ←——————————————→ 0%
always   usually   often   sometimes   never

> Adverbs of frequency go before the main verb.
> *She often* goes *swimming.*
> *They always* have *lunch at 1 o'clock.*
> **BUT** they go after the verb *be*.
> *It is usually cold in the winter.*
> *We* are *never in bed at 9 o'clock.*

Unit 2
present continuous

We use **present continuous** to talk about actions that are happening now, at or around the moment when we speak. We form the present continuous with **am**, **are** or **is** and the main verb with **-ing**.
I am reading *a good book at the moment.*
We are learning *about the weather in today's lesson.*
Oh no! It's raining *again!*

We form the negative by adding the word **not** after **am/are/is**. The short forms are the same as for the verb **be**.
I'm not feeling *very well.*
You aren't listen*ing!*
My webcam isn't work*ing properly.*

Affirmative			
I'm You're/We're/They're He's/She's/It's	(I am) (You/We/They are) (He/She/It is)	studying	now.
Negative			
I'm not (I am not) You/We/They aren't (are not) He/She/It isn't (is not)		studying	now.

We make questions in present continuous by putting **Am/Are/Is** before the subject, and then the main verb with **-ing**.
Am I *making a lot of noise?*
Are you *listening to me?*
Is it *snowing in your town today?*

In short answers we use **am/'m not, are/aren't** or **is/isn't**. We DON'T use the main verb.

Questions		
Am Are Is	I you/we/they he/she/it	reading?
Short answers		

Yes,	I am. you/we/they are. he/she/it is.	No,	I'm not. you/we/they aren't. he/she/it isn't.

present simple and present continuous

We use the **present simple** to talk about things that someone *usually (often/always/etc)* does, and we use the **present continuous** to talk about actions that are happening *now*, at or around the time when we are talking.
Fran usually lives in Rome. She's living in Paris at the moment.
My dad works in a shop. He isn't working today – it's Sunday.

Unit 3
past simple *be*

The past simple of the verb *be* is **was** and **were**.
I was quite good at acting when I was a young child.
He/She/It was the star of the film.
You/We/They were excited about going to see the movie.

The negative is **was not** (**wasn't**) or **were not** (**weren't**).
I wasn't interested in watching the TV show.
He/She/It wasn't very good in that movie.
You/We/They weren't alive in 1964.

Affirmative		
I You/We/They He/She/It	was were was	at the cinema last night.
Negative		
I You/We/They He/She/It	wasn't (was not) weren't (were not) wasn't (was not)	on the Internet yesterday.

past simple (regular and irregular verbs)

We use the **past simple** to talk about actions, events, situations or habits in the past. We form the past simple of regular verbs by adding -ed to the verb. This is the same for all subjects.
I/You/He/She/It/We/They watched *a great film last night.*
I/You/He/She/It/We/They looked *for information on the Internet.*

Irregular verbs DON'T form the past simple by adding **-ed**. They have a different past form.

Present:	come	do	get	go	have	make	see
Past:	came	did	got	went	had	made	saw

*See the **Irregular Verbs** list at the back of the book.*

The **negative** of the past simple is **did not** and the bare infinitive of the main verb. This is the same for regular and irregular verbs, and the same for all subjects. The short form is **didn't**.
I/You/He/She/We/They didn't want *to watch the TV show.*
I/You/He/She/We/They didn't find *any information in the magazine.*

Negative			
I/You/We/They He/She/It	didn't (did not)	know	the answer.

past simple question form (*was*/*were*)

We make questions with **be** in the past simple by putting **was** or **were** before the subject.
Was I good in the school concert?
Were you/we/they alive when Spielberg made Jaws?
Was he/she sad at the end of Titanic?
Was it a good film?

Question		
Was Were Was	I you/we/they he/she/it	at the cinema last night?
Short answers					

Yes,	I you/we/they he/she/it	was. were. was.	No,	I you/we/they he/she/it	wasn't. weren't. wasn't.

past simple question form (*did*)

We make questions in the past simple by putting **Did** before the subject, and then the bare infinitive of the main verb. This is the same for regular and irregular verbs, and the same for all subjects.
Did I/we/he do something wrong?
Did you enjoy the musical?
Did he/she/they go to the cinema?

In short answers, we use **did** or **didn't**. We DON'T use the main verb.

Questions			
Did	I/you/we/they/he/she/it	send	an email?
Short answers			

Yes,	I you/we/they he/she/it	did.	No,	I you/we/they he/she/it	didn't.

past simple questions with *Wh-* words

We can use **question words** to ask for information. We begin with the question word, followed by **was/were** or **did**.
What was Spielberg's first film? – Firelight.
When did he make it? – In 1964.
What time did the film start? – At 8 o'clock.
Where were you yesterday? – At home.
Why was Star Wars successful? – It used amazing special effects.

Most question words begin with **Wh-** but we can also use *How*, *How much/many*, *How long*, etc.
How did they do the special effects? – They used computers.
How many times did you see the film? – Three.
How much money did the film make? – $1.8 billion.

-*ing* and -*ed* adjectives

When something makes a person feel excitement, surprise, interest, etc, we use -**ing adjectives** to describe the thing, and -**ed** adjectives to describe the person.
The lesson was interesting.   *I was interested.*
The film was frightening.   *We were frightened.*
The programme was boring.   *They were bored.*

Unit 4
past continuous

We use **past continuous** to talk about actions that were happening at a particular time in the past.
I was playing football at 4 o'clock this afternoon.

We form the past continuous with **was/were** and the main verb with -**ing**.
We were lying on the beach at this time yesterday.
He was sitting in the garden when I saw him.

With verbs ending in a **consonant + -e**, we change the -**e** to -**ing**.
cha**se**   chasing   sha**ke**   shaking
With most verbs ending in a **single vowel + a consonant**, we double the consonant and add -**ing**.
w**in**   winning   g**et**   getting
With verbs ending in -**ie**, we change the -**ie** to -**ying**.
l**ie**   lying   d**ie**   dying

We form the negative with **wasn't/weren't**.
I wasn't feeling very well at lunchtime.
I told you, but you weren't listening!

Affirmative			
I/He/She/It You/We/They	was were	sleeping	at 3 a.m.
Negative			
I/He/She/It You/We/They	wasn't weren't	(was not) (were not)	sleeping at 3 a.m.

We make questions in past continuous by putting **Was/Were** before the subject, and then the main verb with -**ing**.
Were you watching the news on TV at nine o'clock?
Was it raining when you left for school?

In short answers we use *was/wasn't* or *were/weren't*. We DON'T use the main verb.

Questions			
Was Were	I/he/she/it you/we/they	sleeping	at 3 a.m.?
Short answers			
Yes,	I/he/she/it you/we/they	was. were.	No,	I/he/she/it you/we/they	wasn't. weren't.

past simple and past continuous

We use **past continuous** for an action that was already happening at the time a second action happened or began; we use **past simple** for the second action.
They were driving to London (past continuous) when the accident happened. (past simple).

We use *when* + **past simple** OR *while* + **past continuous** to talk about the two actions together.
I was having a bath (past continuous) when the phone rang. (past simple).
The phone rang (past simple) while I was having a bath. (past continuous)

We can put the two actions in any order, but we must still use *when* + **past simple** OR *while* + **past continuous**.
When the phone rang, (past simple) I was having a bath. (past continuous)
While I was having a bath, (past continuous) the phone rang. (past simple)

Unit 5
comparative adjectives

We use **comparative adjectives** to compare two people, animals or things. We form the comparative with **adjective + -er + than** or **more/less + adjective + than**.
An elephant is bigger than a tiger.
A lion is more dangerous than a giraffe.
English is less difficult than Chinese.

• **adjectives with one syllable**
With one-syllable adjectives, we form the comparative by adding **-er**.
long – longer
If the adjective ends in **-e**, we just add **-r**.
clos**e** – closer
If the adjective ends in a **single vowel + consonant**, we double the consonant and add **-er**.
b**ig** – bigger
• **adjectives with -y**
With adjectives ending in **-y**, we change the **-y** to **-ier**.
dr**y** – drier   prett**y** – prettier
• **adjectives with two or more syllables**
With other adjectives of two or more syllables, we form the comparative by adding **more** or **less** before the adjective.
boring – more/less boring
exciting – more/less exciting
interesting – more/less interesting
• **irregular adjectives**
There are some irregular adjectives that don't follow the rules above.
good – better
bad – worse
many, much – more
a lot of, lots of – more
little – less

too, (not) enough

We use **too** + adjective or **not** + adjective + **enough** to explain why something is/was not possible. The main verb is in *to* + **infinitive**.
Ben is young, so he can't drive a car.   [young = not old]
Ben is too young to drive a car.   *Ben isn't old enough to drive a car.*

superlative adjectives

We use **superlative adjectives** to compare one person, animal or thing with two or more others. We form the superlative with **the** + **adjective** + **-est** or **the most/least** + **adjective**. We can use **in the world**, **of all**, etc after the noun.
The giraffe is the tallest animal in the world.
This is the most poisonous snake of all.

• **adjectives with one syllable**
With one-syllable adjectives, we form the superlative by adding **the ...-est**.
cold – the coldest
With adjectives ending in **-e**, we just add **the ...-st**.
nic**e** – the nicest
With adjectives ending in a **single vowel + consonant**, we double the consonant and add **the ...-est**.
b**ig** – the biggest
• **adjectives with -y**
With adjectives ending in **-y**, we change the **-y** to **the ...-iest**.
dr**y** – the driest   ugl**y** – the ugliest
• **adjectives with two or more syllables**
With other adjectives of two or more syllables, we form the comparative by adding **the most** or **the least** before the adjective.
boring – the most/least boring
amazing – the most/least amazing
interesting – the most/least interesting
• **irregular adjectives**
There are some irregular adjectives that don't follow the rules above.
good – the best
bad – the worst
many, much – the most
a lot of, lots of – the most
a little – the least

have to

We use **have to** to talk about what is/isn't necessary.
Divers have to be careful of sharks.

We form the affirmative with **have/has to** and the bare infinitive of the main verb.
Rock climbers have to be brave and strong.
A doctor has to study for years and years.

We form the negative with **don't/doesn't** + **have to** + the bare infinitive of the main verb.
You don't have to be tough to enjoy jogging.
Adam doesn't have to go to bed early on Friday.

Affirmative			
I/You/We/They He/She/It	have to has to		buy new boots.
Negative			
I/You/We/They He/She/It	don't doesn't	have to	buy new boots.

We make questions by putting **Do/Does** before the subject, and then **have to** + the bare infinitive of the main verb.
Do I have to tidy **my room?**
Does Kate have to go **to the doctor?**

In short answers we use **do/don't** or **does/doesn't**. We DON'T use the main verb.

Questions			
Do Does	I/you/we/they he/she/it	have to	make breakfast?
Short answers					
---	---	---	---	---	---
Yes,	I/you/we/they he/she/it	do. is.	No,	you/we/they he/she/it	don't. doesn't.

Unit 6
must/mustn't

We use **must** to talk about what the rules/laws/etc tell us to do.
You must wear a helmet on a motorbike.

Must has the same form for all subjects (I, you, he, etc). The main verb after **must** is in the **bare infinitive**.
I/We/She/etc must be **quiet in the classroom.**

The negative of **must** is **mustn't** (must not) and it is the same for all subjects.

> **Musn't** DOESN'T mean something is not necessary; it means something is against the rules/law (i.e. not permitted).
> **You don't have to cycle to school – you can walk.** [It's not necessary.]
> **You mustn't cycle on the walkway.** [It's not permitted.]

Affirmative		
I/You/He/She/ It/We/They	must	wear a seat belt.
Negative		
I/You/He/She/ It/We/They	mustn't (must not)	walk on the grass.

can/can't and must/mustn't

We use **Can** to ask what is/isn't permitted; in short answers we use **can** or **can't**.
Can we park our car here?
   - No, you can't. You mustn't park here. You must park outside.
Can I take a photo?
   - No, you can't. You mustn't take photos in the museum.

countable and uncountable nouns

Countable nouns are nouns we can count – e.g. **one camera** (singular), **two cameras** (plural). When the subject is plural, the verb is also plural.
This camera **is expensive. Those** cameras **are cheap.**

Uncountable nouns are nouns we can't count (**food, milk,** etc). They haven't got a plural form. When the subject is an uncountable noun, the verb is singular.
This food **is fresh.**

> We don't use **a** or **an** with uncountable nouns or plural nouns.

We can use countable words like a **piece**, a **bottle**, a **cup**, a **glass**, a **carton**, etc to show how much there is of something uncountable.
That's a **big piece of meat.**
Two **cups of coffee, please!**

some, any and no

In **affirmative** sentences, we use **some** before countable nouns in the plural and before uncountable nouns.
There were some biscuits **on the plate.**
There was some food **in the kitchen.**

In **negative** sentences and **questions**, we use **any** before countable nouns in the plural and before uncountable nouns.
There weren't any trees **at the top of the mountain.**
We didn't take any water **with us.**
Did you see any lions **at the zoo?**
Were there any people **in the room?**
Was there any milk **in the fridge?**

In negative sentences, we can use **no** in the same way as **not any**.
There were **no mobile phones 50 years ago.** [= There weren't any ...]
I wanted to buy it, but I had **no money.** [= I didn't have any ...]

Unit 7
present perfect (affirmative/negative)

We use the **present perfect** to talk about actions in the recent past, but we don't know or don't mention exactly when the action happened.

I have cleaned my room, Mum!   [one minute ago? one hour ago?]

We form the present perfect with **have** or **has** and the **past participle** of the main verb. With regular verbs, the past participle is the bare infinitive + **-ed**.
I've (have) pack**ed my suitcase.**
Judy's mum has cook**ed dinner for us.**

Irregular verbs DON'T form the past participle by adding **-ed**. They have a different past participle form. Example:

Infinitive	Past	Past participle
be	was/were	been
come	came	come
do	did	done

I've sent Kezia a text message about the party.
Someone has stolen that woman's purse.

126

We form the negative with **haven't** or **hasn't** and the past participle of the main verb.
I haven't done my homework, but I'll do it later.
He hasn't checked his emails today.

Affirmative		
I/You/ We/They He/She/It	've (have) 's (has)	eaten breakfast.
Negative		
I/You/ We/They He/She/It	haven't (have not) hasn't (has not)	eaten breakfast.

present perfect (questions, short answers and *ever*)

We make present perfect questions by putting **Have/Has** before the subject, and then the past participle of the main verb. In short answers we use **have/has** or **haven't/hasn't**. We DON'T use the main verb.

We can use the word **ever** in present perfect questions; it always goes before the main verb.
Have you ever been skydiving?
Has Lewis ever visited your grandparents?

Questions		
Have Has	I/you/we/they he/she/it	(ever) been late for school?
Short answers		
Yes,	I/you/we/they he/she/it	have. has.	No,	I/you/we/they he/she/it	haven't. hasn't.

present perfect with *never*

We can form negative sentences in the present perfect with the word **never**; it always goes before the main verb.
We have never been to Brazil.
He has never stolen any money.

Unit 8
will

We use **will** to talk about predictions about the future. We often use *will* after *I think, I hope, I'm sure*, etc.
I think it will be hot tomorrow.
I'm sure people will live on the moon in 2110.

Will has the same form for all subjects (*I, you, he*, etc). The main verb after **will** is in the **bare infinitive**.
I/We/She/etc will have a great time at the party.

The negative of **will** is **won't** (will not) and it is the same for all subjects.

We make questions by putting **Will** before the subject, and then the bare infinitive of the main verb. In short answers we use **will** or **won't**. We DON'T use the main verb.

Affirmative		
I/You/He/ She/It/ We/They	'll (will)	be a success.
Negative		
I/You/He/ She/It/ We/They	won't (will not)	be a success.
Questions		
Will	I/you/he/she/ it/we/they	be a success?
Short answers					
Yes,	I/you/he/ she/it/ we/they	will.	No,	I/you/he/ she/it/ we/they	won't.

first conditional

We use the **first conditional** to talk about future actions or predictions based on a *condition* – that is, another future event where two things are possible.

Will it be hot tomorrow? → YES We'll go swimming.
→ NO We'll stay at home.

If it is hot tomorrow, we'll go swimming.
If it isn't hot tomorrow, we'll stay at home.

> We form the first conditional with **If + present simple** for the condition, followed by **will/won't** for the second future action or prediction. We <u>don't</u> use **will/won't** for the condition.
> *If it rains [NOT If it will rain] tomorrow, I'll take an umbrella.*
> *If they feel [NOT If they will feel] tired, they won't go to the cinema.*
> *If you don't take [NOT If you won't take] a map, you'll get lost.*

going to and the present continuous

We use **will** to talk about the future when we have just decided what to do, at the time of speaking, but haven't really made any plans.
Where can I go on holiday? I know – I'll go to Turkey.

We use **be going to** to talk about the future when we have already decided what to do, and have made some plans.
I'm going to go to Turkey this summer. I found some nice places on the Internet.

We use the **present continuous** to talk about the future when we have made more exact plans and arrangements (e.g. bought tickets, arranged to meet someone, etc). When we use the present continuous in this way, we say the time or date.
I'm going to Turkey on 15 July. I've booked a package holiday.

> Be careful with **be going to go** and **be going** (Present continuous).
> *I'm going to go shopping later.* (going to)
> *I'm going to Paris next Tuesday.* (present continuous)

English Explorer Student's Book 2
Helen Stephenson

Publisher: Jason Mann

Adaptations Manager: Alistair Baxter

Assistant Editor: Manuela Barros

Technology Development Manager: Debie Mirtle

Product and Marketing Manager: Ruth McAleavey

Senior Content Project Editor: Natalie Griffith

Senior Production Controller: Paul Herbert

National Geographic Liaison: Leila Hishmeh

Art Director: Natasa Arsenidou

Cover/Text Designer: Natasa Arsenidou

Compositor: Sophia Ioannidou and PreMedia Global

Audio: EFS Television Production Ltd

Acknowledgements

The publisher would like to thank Robert Crossley for writing the True Story and Project pages.

The Publisher would also like to thank the following for their invaluable contribution: Nick Sheard, Karen Spiller and Liz Driscoll.

ISBN: 978-1-111-06187-6

National Geographic Learning
Cheriton House
North Way
Andover
Hampshire
SP10 5BE
United Kingdom

Cengage Learning is a leading provider of customized learning solutions with office locations around the globe, including Singapore, the United Kingdom, Australia, Mexico, Brazil and Japan. Locate your local office at:
international.cengage.com/region

Cengage Learning products are represented in Canada by Nelson Education, Ltd.

Visit National Geographic Learning online at **ngl.cengage.com**
Visit our corporate website at **www.cengage.com**

Photo credits
The publishers would like to thank the following sources for permission to reproduce their copyright protected photographs:
Cover photo: (Alaska Stock Images / National Geographic Image Collection)
pp 4 (Shutterstock.com), 5 (Shutterstock.com), 5 (Shutterstock.com), 8 (Shutterstock.com), 8 (Shutterstock.com), 11 (Tomasz Tomaszewski/National Geographic Image Collection), 12 (Reza/National Geographic Image Collection), 12 (Yuri Arcurs/Fotolia.com), 12 (Australia flag) (Shutterstock.com), 12 (Afghanistan flag)(Shutterstock.com), 12 (students) (Shutterstock.com), 14 (Jodi Cobb/National Geographic Image Collection), 14 (Jodi Cobb/National Geographic Image Collection), 15 (Jodi Cobb/National Geographic Image Collection), 16 (brick wall) (Shutterstock.com), 17 (website) (Shutterstock.com), 18 (grahamheywood/iStockphoto.com), 19 (Aleksandra Kurcman/iStockphoto.com), 20 (background) (Shutterstock.com), 21 (Mark Thiessen/National Geographic Image Collection), 22 (Harold F. Pierce/NASA/National Geographic Image Collection), 24 (Gordon Wiltsie/National Geographic Image Collection), 24 (Gordon Wiltsie/National Geographic Image Collection), 24 (Gordon Wiltsie/National Geographic Image Collection), 27 (message pad) (Shutterstock.com), 28 (Paul Nicklen/National Geographic Image Collection), 28 (Norbert Rosing/National Geographic Image Collection), 29 (PixelsAway/BigStockPhoto.com), 29 (jnnfrws/BigStockPhoto.com), 29 (Adventure_Photo/iStockphoto.com), 31 (Cathy Yeulet/123rf.com), 32 (Shutterstock.com), 32 (Shutterstock.com), 32 (Shutterstock.com), 32 (Shutterstock.com), 33 (background) (Shutterstock.com), 33 (izusek/iStockphoto.com), 34 (Kenneth Garrett/National Geographic Image Collection), 34 (Keenpress/National Geographic Image Collection), 34 (parchment) (Shutterstock.com), 36 (Shutterstock.com), 36 (Shutterstock.com), 36 (TebNad/BigStockPhoto.com), 38 (bottom) (Shutterstock.com), 38 (background) (Shutterstock.com), 40 (badboo/BigStockPhoto.com), 40 (curaphotography/BigStockPhoto.com), 40 (Julianna Tilton/Fotolia.com), 40 (JLV Image Works/Fotolia.com), 40 (YM/epa/Corbis), 41 (Trevor/BigStockPhoto.com), 42 (Shutterstock.com), 42 (Shutterstock.com), 42 (Shutterstock.com), 43 (Bates Littlehales/National Geographic Image Collection), 44 courtesy of Joseph Lekuton), 44 (Richard Du Toit/Minden Pictures/National Geographic Image Collection), 46 (Bill Curtsinger/National Geographic Image Collection), 46 (Shutterstock.com), 48 (Shutterstock.com), 48 (background) (Shutterstock.com), 49 (Sarah Leen/National Geographic Image Collection), 49 (Bettmann/Corbis), 49 (film strip) (Shutterstock.com), 50 (Urbanmyth/Alamy), 50 (Charles Allmon/National Geographic Image Collection), 50 (Jason Edwards/National Geographic Image Collection), 53 (robert lerich/Fotolia.com), 54 (Shutterstock.com), 54 (Shutterstock.com), 54 (Shutterstock.com), 55 (Tim Laman/National Geographic Image Collection), 56 (Richard du Toit/Minden Pictures/National Geographic Image Collection), 56 (background) (Shutterstock.com), 58 (Stephen Alvarez/National Geographic Image Collection), 58 (Shutterstock.com), 58 (Shutterstock.com), 58 (Shutterstock.com), 62 (Konrad Wothe/Minden Pictures/National Geographic Image Collection), 62 (EcoView/Fotolia.com), 62 (GP232/iStockphoto.com), 62 (Frans Lanting/National Geographic Image Collection), 63 (Shutterstock.com), 64 (Shutterstock.com), 64 (Shutterstock.com), 64 (NVB/Wikimedia Commons), 65 (Rich Reid/National Geographic Image Collection), 66 (RacingThePlanet Limited), 68 (Barry Bishop/National Geographic Image Collection), 70 (inset) (Shutterstock.com), 70 (inset) (Shutterstock.com), 71 (Shutterstock.com), 72 (matejmm/iStockphoto.com), 72 (Nano/Fotolia.com), 73 (Speedfighter/BigStockPhoto.com), 73 (mavrick/BigStockPhoto.com), 73 (Shutterstock.com), 76 (Shutterstock.com), 77 (Taylor S. Kennedy/National Geographic Image Collection), 79 (Shutterstock.com), 80 (Cathy Yeulet/123rf.com), 80 (Don Mason/Brand X/Corbis), 80 (John Eastcott and Yva Momatiuk/National Geographic Image Collection), 82 (Shutterstock.com), 83 (stationery) (Shutterstock.com), 84 (Robert Clark/National Geographic Image Collection), 84 (Sisse Brimberg/National Geographic Image Collection), 84 (Robert Clark/National Geographic Image Collection), 86 (Beverly Joubert/National Geographic Image Collection), 86 (background, bottom, bottom right) (Shutterstock.com), 87 (Alaska Stock Images/National Geographic Image Collection), 88 (NASA/National Geographic Image Collection), 88 (Murray Andrew/Corbis Sygma), 88 (Shutterstock.com), 90 (honster/iStockphoto.com), 93 (Shutterstock.com), 93 (Shutterstock.com), 94 (iStockphoto.com/monkeybusinessimages), 114 (Shutterstock.com), 115 (Shutterstock.com), 115 (iStockphoto.com/jeremkin), 116 (Shutterstock.com), 117 (Shutterstock.com), 118 (Shutterstock.com), 119 (Shutterstock.com), 120 (Shutterstock.com), 121 (Shutterstock.com)

The following photographs were taken on commission © Heinle, Cengage Learning by MM Studios Ltd. pp 4–5, 7–8, 16–17, 26–27, 38–39, 48, 60, 70, 82–83, 92

Illustrations by Nigel Dobbyn pp 51, 52, 61, 96, 102, 106, 112; Panagiotis Angeletakis pp 10; Dylan Gibson pp 13, 30, 45, 74, 78, 92, 98, 101, 105, 110; Celia Hart pp 22, 26, 36, 57, 74, 91, 100, 104, 107, 109, 111 t; Tim Kahane pp 16, 19; Martin Sanders pp 24, 41, 51, 63; Eric Smith pp 23, 66, 81, 99, 103 b, 108, 111 b; Mark Turner pp 67, 102, 113

Printed in Greece by Bakis SA
Print Number: 08   Print Year: 2016